Profit from
the Evening News

Profit from the Evening News

the Evening News

Using Leading Economic Indicators
to Make Smart Money Decisions

Marie Bussing-Burks
M.B.A., D.A.

SOURCEBOOKS, INC.®
NAPERVILLE, ILLINOIS

Copyright © 2001 by Marie Bussing-Burks
Cover design © 2001 by Sourcebooks, Inc.
Cover image © 2001 Robin Jareaux/Artville

This publication is designed to provide accurate and authoritative information in regard to the subject matter covered. It is sold with the understanding that the publisher is not engaged in rendering legal, accounting, or other professional service. If legal advice or other expert assistance is required, the services of a competent professional person should be sought.—*From a Declaration of Principles Jointly Adopted by a Committee of the American Bar Association and a Committee of Publishers and Associations*

Trademarks: All brand names and product names used in this book are trademarks, registered trademarks, or trade names of their respective holders. Sourcebooks, Inc., is not associated with any product or vendor in this book.

Published by Sourcebooks, Inc.
P.O. Box 4410, Naperville, Illinois 60567-4410
(630) 961-3900
FAX: (630) 961-2168

Library of Congress Cataloging-in-Publication Data

Bussing-Burks, Marie, 1958–
    Profit from the evening news: using leading economic indicators to make smart money decisions / Marie Bussing-Burks.
        p. cm
    Includes bibliographical references and index.
    ISBN 1-57071-587-4 (alk. paper)
    1. Finance, Personal—United States. 2. Economic indicators—United States. I. Title.

HG179 .B8765 2001
332.024—dc21

                                                          00-066161

Printed and bound in the United States of America
        DO   10 9 8 7 6 5 4 3 2 1

To my parents,
Connie and Bud Bussing

Contents

Acknowledgments ix

1. Winning with Economic Indicators 1

2. Take the Lead: Our Top Nine Indicators 7

3. The Big Picture: Gross Domestic Product 13

4. A Good Time to Job Hunt?
   Unemployment Insurance Claims 29

5. Bargain Shopping? *Durable Goods Orders* 43

6. Move or Redecorate? *Building Permits* 55

7. Investing in 90 Percent of the Market: *S&P 500* 71

8. Easy or Tight? *M2 Money Supply* 85

9. Is It a Good Time to Open a Business?
   Corporate Profits after Tax .99

10. An Early Warning Signal: *Federal Funds Rate* 111

11. Buy Now, Pay Later: *The Yield Curve* 129

12. Inside Information: *Leading Economic Indicator* 141

13. Make Smart Money Decisions 157

Appendix 163

Notes 165

Bibliography 171

Index 175

About the Author 181

Acknowledgments

Writing this book has been a collaborative effort involving input from many people. It is with much appreciation that I acknowledge their assistance.

My thanks go to Melinda Gingerich, a business student in economics at the University of Southern Indiana. The charts she designed help dramatize the movements of the indicators around the business cycle. Her graphic skills are top-notch.

I am grateful to Jacinto L. Torres, Jr., Business Cycle Analyst, Economics Program, The Conference Board; and Matthew Cottell, Business Cycle Indicator (BCI) Program Coordinator, The Conference Board. Both were helpful in answering numerous questions involving The Conference Board's extensive BCI database.

A large amount of data from government agencies was used in this book. I am grateful to Lee Wentela, M3, U.S. Census Bureau; Maria Romain, Residential Construction Division, U.S. Census Bureau; Cindy Ambler, Employment and Training Division, U.S. Department of Labor; and Kenneth Petrick, Bureau of Economic Analysis, U.S. Department of Commerce. They provided valuable insights about their agencies' data.

In addition, I am indebted to those in the newspaper and television media for alerting me to the publication trend for the indicators in this book. A special thanks to Connie Ford, Economics Editor of *The Wall Street Journal;* Sandra Block, Personal Financial Reporter for *USA Today;* and Louis Uchitelle, Business and Financial Reporter for *The New York Times.*

Finally, I owe special thanks to my editor at Sourcebooks, Deborah Werksman. Her talent, guidance, and contributions were invaluable.

Her assistant, Elizabeth Meagher, was always available for help.

My thanks to all who assisted with writing this book.

I acknowledge my family, to whom I owe a debt of gratitude for their support and enthusiasm. Thank you to my parents, Connie and Bud Bussing; my husband, Barry Burks; and our daughters, Annemarie and Katie.

Chapter 1

Winning with Economic Indicators

"I believe the true road to preeminent success in any line is to make yourself master of that line."

—Andrew Carnegie

As a kid, you probably had a lemonade stand, and an allowance, and maybe you took an economics or a home economics course in high school or college. Now that you are an adult, responsible for your own finances, do you wish you knew more about how money works, so you could make smart money decisions?

It is easier than you think. Your money fits into the big picture of the country's economy. By keeping an eye on some of the indicators that economists use to predict the direction the economy is going, you will be able to make smarter financial decisions in every area of your life. Your timing will be better, your investments will be more profitable, your borrowing less costly, and your grasp of money matters more skillful. This book explains nine easy-to-follow indicators that will help you make money decisions in all areas of your life: 1) unemployment insurance claims, 2) durable goods orders, 3) building permits, 4) S&P 500, 5) M2 money supply, 6) corporate profits after tax, 7) federal funds rate, 8) yield curve, and 9) leading economic indicator.

One indicator provides a quick peek at future overall economic activity, to give you broad hints for all your money moves. The other indicators shed light on specific money decisions: career choices, buying big-ticket items (such as appliances, cars, and computers), investing in stocks and bonds, buying or selling a home, borrowing, or starting a business. You may have an interest in all of these money areas or perhaps only a few of them apply to your life. You can choose only those indicators you will want to follow, or track all nine indicators for a complete overview of all your money matters.

Each chapter provides a definition of one indicator and explains to which financial area it is relevant. You will also find out how far ahead of recessions and expansions the indicator moves, and my recommendation on how long to track the indicator to have enough information to use that indicator to its best effect. A chart at the end of the chapter will help you track your own money. In addition, you'll find out where to look for each indicator; when and how the indicator is compiled; how the financial markets (primarily the stock market and the bond market) react to each indicator; and more in-depth information for those who wish to know more.

The Indicators

Economists use leading economic indicators to predict when economic activity will rise or fall. Each of the nine indicators, discussed in chapters 4 through 12, provides an early hint on economic good or bad times. Consequently, each indicator allows you to address specific money issues early on in the four-phase business cycle (recession, trough, expansion, and peak—see Chart 3-2). Chapter 2 has a detailed summary of each indicator, but here is a quick overview of each:

- **Unemployment Insurance Claims.** The number of new claims filed for unemployment insurance. You'll want to track this number for job and career decisions.

- **Durable Goods Orders.** Durable goods are big-ticket items with an expected life of one year or more, such as cars, furniture, computers, electronics, home appliances, medical supplies, and aircraft. This indictor tracks orders for such goods placed with domestic manufacturers. This number will be useful for timing expensive purchases.

- **Building Permits.** The number of new private homes authorized for construction by local building permits. Building permits is the number to track to make smart decisions about home ownership and moving.

- **S&P 500.** A stock market index composed of 500 blue-chip stocks, representing all key business industries. This index number is relevant to your stock investment portfolio.

☛ **M2 Money Supply.** This represents the total dollar amount of coin, currency, traveler's checks, checking accounts, savings deposits, money market deposit accounts, small CDs, repurchase agreements, and small money market mutual funds. While this is a little more difficult to find than the other indicators, M2 money supply is worth tracking when you are borrowing or otherwise working with debt.

☛ **Corporate Profits After Tax.** The after-tax profits of public and private corporate enterprises. Also a little less widely reported, this is the number you'll want to track if you're thinking about starting or buying a business.

☛ **Federal Funds.** This indicator, which shows the interest rate on money that is borrowed overnight between banks, is the number to watch when investing in bonds.

☛ **Yield Curve.** Track this spread between short-term and long-term interest rates to make the best decisions about credit and financing.

☛ **Leading Economic Indicator (LEI).** This measurement is a consolidation of ten individual indicators. The LEI gives you a sense of the general direction of the economy so that you can plan ahead in all areas of your money.

These nine indicators were chosen not only because of their predictive record but because they are relatively easy to find. Most are reported widely. You will likely catch them on the evening news, on the radio, or in your local paper. But if you miss them, you can find most in *USA Today, The Wall Street Journal,* or *Investor's Business Daily.* The two exceptions to this are M2 money supply, which requires a little more digging but is worth the effort if you're in the market for a loan or refinancing; and corporate profits, which will help you with starting up or buying a small business. If you're interested in doing more in-depth research, you can also find all of these indicators and related information on the Internet (Web site addresses are provided), and many of these numbers are available by telephoning recorded messages as well.

The final chapter reviews how these numbers can help you make the most astute decisions—those that will maximize your long-term wealth. The tracking chart provided in the Appendix lists all the indicators—plus when and where to find them—and gives you a place to record the numbers as you track the indicators.

Measure Economic Activity

To see how it works, let's first look at how economy-wide activity is measured. The main benchmark of overall economic spending is gross domestic product (GDP). GDP is the final value of all goods and services produced for sale during the year. In the United States we spend more than $9 trillion—yes, $9,000,000,000,000—on a vast multitude of new products each year: automobiles, furniture, wide-screen television sets, food, clothing, haircuts, dental visits, and so forth. Fluctuations in GDP are the most important benchmarks of economic advance or decline and form the pattern of the nation's business cycle. In chapter 3 we examine the big picture, GDP, as the ultimate measurement of economic performance.

The lows and highs in economic activity are called recessions and expansions. A downturn is a period of time during which the total real GDP of the economy declines. As a rule of thumb, if a downturn in economic activity lasts more than two consecutive quarters (i.e., longer than six-months), it becomes a recession. In a recession, the economy is doing poorly. Business activity is sluggish, and many individuals are unemployed.

An upturn, or expansion, is when real GDP rises. In an expansion, the economy is performing well. Government officials, business executives, and consumers are pleased about the state of the economy. There are a lot of job opportunities; business is booming.

The National Bureau of Economic Research (NBER), a private research group in Cambridge, Massachusetts, began researching business cycles in the late 1920s; by the mid-1930s it began determining the country's official recessions and expansions. NBER does such a top-notch job at pinpointing highs and lows in the economy that even the U.S. government has adopted NBER's dates as the official periods of recessions and expansions. According to NBER's business cycle dates, since April 1960 the country has experienced five complete business cycles. The average recession has lasted over eleven months, while expansions have run much longer—an average of slightly more than sixty months. And although, at this writing the economy is slowing, the United States is still experiencing the longest expansion in history—over nine full years of solid GDP growth. But we know a downturn will occur eventually. History tells us that business cycles are an endless succession of ups and downs in the economy. Recessions are just like the common cold. They come and they go. There is nothing we can do about them. But wouldn't it be helpful to know when one will occur so you could prepare?

Watching economic indicators can help you prepare by forecasting which direction the economy is going. There are actually three types of forecasting indicators: 1) leading, 2) coincident, and 3) lagging. The name given to each refers to the way the indicator moves in relation to changes in overall economic activity.

Leading indicators can be used to forecast economic activity because they tell us what is likely to happen a few months from now. Leading indicators are economic statistics that change in a definite direction prior to a rise or fall in economic activity. The indicators in this book are all leaders, so you can plan your money moves, and plan early.

Coincident indicators, useful for verifying forecasts, turn at the same time the economy moves.

Lagging indicators are very belated because they move in a direction after the economy has already shifted.

Making predictions about future general economic conditions with leading indicators is the basis for making many decisions in government and business. Why not use it for your own money decisions?

Heads Up on Money Decisions

Because these indicators are leading the economy, tracking them allows you to start to plan your money strategies months before the economy has actually entered bad times or good times.

In addition, monitoring economic statistics isn't limited to reading the paper or watching the news. You can verify your assessment of what the economic indicators are telling you by tuning into all kinds of conversations around you. Having lunch tomorrow with your sister, the town's hotshot real estate agent? Be sure to quiz her about the housing industry. Is there much new construction in town? How does she feel about the national trend of new home construction? Assuming the building permits index has bottomed out and sis has a doomsday projection for the entire industry, you have reinforced the signal of this indicator. You have, no doubt, further increased your suspicion of an upcoming recession. Plus, you now know that some great homes will be for sale in the upcoming months as people find it difficult to keep up with their mortgage payments.

It is Friday night and you are at the company's stuffy annual dinner party. Tonight, you score and get to sit at the table with the bigwigs. After a few cocktails, the president of the company begins to talk about how stellar the firm's soon-to-be-released profit figures are and how they will take Wall Street off-guard. You remember that over the last few quarters, corporate profits after tax has been on the upswing. The president's words and your reading reinforce the indication of a strong corporate environment, which is great for the economy's continued expansion. In a strong corporate business atmosphere, business profits universally swell. You are now sure it's a good time to start that small side business you and your spouse have been thinking about.

Using indicators is that simple. It is fun to think about, analyze, and interpret the statistics once they are demystified and you know where to find them and how to apply them.

Chapter 2

Take the Lead: Our Top Nine Indicators

"A leader is a dealer in hope."

—Napoleon Bonaparte

There are a number of leading economic indicators. Most are commonly known or understood in the economics profession. Often, however, you will find debate on indicators—do they lead, coincide with, or lag economic activity? All of the series you'll read about in this book are clearly leaders. I have chosen them for that quality, so that if you follow them for a period of time, you will be better informed about which way the economy is headed.

Following is a brief summary of each indicator reviewed in this book. Seeing how each series relates to the overall business cycle provides a sense of the foretelling strength of these nine indicators:

1. **Unemployment Insurance Claims:** The Employment and Training Administration (ETA) of the U.S. Department of Labor releases the number of new applications for unemployment insurance filed each week. When the number of new claims starts to pick up, tough times are ahead for the economy. When claims start to fall off, the economy will improve shortly.

2. **Durable Goods Orders:** Originally compiled by the Bureau of the Census, durable goods represents commitments for orders placed with domestic manufacturers. Orders are an important indicator of future business activity because the more orders a manufacturer receives, the more inclined it is to increase production.

Heightened manufacturing production will increase the economy's production. Durable goods is reported monthly; it picks up months before the economy rebounds and falls just before the economy turns down.

3. **Building Permits:** Each month the Bureau of the Census reports the number of new housing units authorized by local building permits. (A building permit is required before building a new home.) The number of building permits is uniquely tied to the economy because it means that money will soon flow to the housing industry, plus many spin-off businesses as new home owners purchase new furniture, appliances, and accessories to fill a new house. Building permits peak months before the economy peaks and begins contracting. Likewise, building permits hit their bottom prior to the economy's bottoming and subsequent expansion.

4. **S&P 500:** The Standard & Poor's composite index represents 500 leading companies. When investors are positive about the economy, they will buy stock, pushing up the market index. Investors anticipating tough business times will sell, pushing the market down. The index skyrockets during a boom period and slumps during a contraction. The index is available on a daily basis.

5. **M2 Money Supply:** The Federal Reserve reports monthly the dollar value of the amount of money being held outside the banking industry. M2 represents the dollar amount of coin, currency, traveler's checks, checkable deposits (check deposits, share drafts, and NOW accounts), savings deposits, money market deposit accounts, small-denomination time deposits, retail repurchase liabilities, and retail money market mutual funds. When this indicator starts to contract and the economy is becoming less liquid, a recession is on the horizon. Before the economy enters an expansion, M2 will rise, a sign of liquidity and strength in the overall economy.

6. **Corporate Profits After Tax:** The Bureau of Economic Analysis (BEA) releases Corporate Profits After Tax—reporting the combined after-tax profits of all incorporated businesses, both public and private. The quarterly series leads contractions and expansions. If the profits of firms are strong, it is a good sign of prosperous times for the overall economy. Likewise, if corporate profits are depressed, the economy is likely headed for tough times.

7. **Federal Funds Rate:** The federal funds (interbank loan) rate fluctuates daily based on current supply and demand of funds. It is influenced by the Federal Reserve System, based upon the expansion or contraction of money. The rate peaks and starts to fall shortly before a recession hits (but lags for an expansion). It is the only interest rate to turn down prior to a recession. All others fall after the economy has entered a contraction. This indicator is reported daily.

8. **Yield Curve:** This curve, published daily, illustrates the difference between long-term rates and short-term rates. When short-term rates become higher than long-term rates, the curve becomes inverted, and a recession generally follows. Conversely, when short-term rates become lower than long-term rates, the curve slopes upward and strong economic activity usually follows.

9. **Leading Economic Indicator:** The Conference Board, a not-for-profit business research organization, produces the monthly leading economic indicator (LEI). This measure of ten composite individual leading economic indicators (four of which are from this list, combined with various other indicators) is useful in predicting both expansions and contractions of the business cycle. It is the most highly watched economic indicator because it is such a handy summary of upcoming economic activity. Negative readings of the LEI suggest a slow economy in the coming months. Positive readings suggest prosperity on the horizon.

How to Use This Book

The nine indicators identified above piece together a complete picture of the economy. Each provides information and is vital in its own right, and as a group, the indicators are a powerful barometer. Keep in mind that you'll want to track each indicator over a period of time before you try to judge what it is telling you about the economy. Convenient charts appear at the end of each chapter as a way to keep your tracking information organized. You can use these economic indicators as a complete source for a better sense of what is happening in the overall economy. Or you can address some of the specific money decisions you may face by checking out select indicators. For a quick overview, Chart 2-1 shows which area of personal finance is addressed by each of the nine indicators.

Chart 2-1

MONEY DECISIONS

Indicator	Check it out if you have any money decisions about	Where to find
Unemployment Insurance Claims	Job and career decisions	Chapter 4
Durable Goods Orders	Big-ticket purchases (appliances, cars, pools, boats)	Chapter 5
Building Permits	Buying, selling, or building a house	Chapter 6
S&P 500	Investments in equity (stocks)	Chapter 7
M2 Money Supply	Credit and financing (obtaining a loan)	Chapter 8
Corporate Profits After Tax	Starting or buying a small business	Chapter 9
Federal Funds Rate	Investing in the bond market	Chapter 10
Yield Curve	Credit and financing (length of loans)	Chapter 11
Leading Economic Indicator	Overall economic shifts	Chapter 12

Money Decisions

The nine economic indicators we'll be examining provide a predictive hint about the economy's business cycle. These leading indicators are used to forecast economic activity a few months from now. So these indicators generally will move up prior to a rise in the economy and usually will fall prior to a fall in overall economic activity (with the exception of unemployment insurance claims, which goes in the opposite direction—rising when the economy falls and falling when the economy booms). They tell us what is going to happen before it happens in the overall economy. Having a sense of what is going on in the economy as a whole will give you a powerful edge to make smart decisions about your own personal finances.

Chapter 3

The Big Picture: Gross Domestic Product

"After all, the chief business of the American people is business."
—Calvin Coolidge

Gross Domestic Product (GDP), while not an economic indicator, is the most important economic measurement available because it is the single best measure of U.S. economic output and spending. GDP reflects the nation's expenditures on all goods and services produced in the calendar year. This single figure provides economists, government officials, businesspeople—and now you—with a measurement of how the economy is doing.

Rather than referring to GDP as an economic indicator, GDP is more appropriately termed an economic benchmark. Strong GDP generally means a growing economy. Weak GDP suggests a depressed economy. The nine economic indicators we'll be examining provide a predictive hint about real GDP (adjusted for inflation) and the economy's business cycle. The nine leading economic indicators, like unemployment insurance claims, durable goods orders, building permits, S&P 500, M2 money supply, corporate profits after tax, the federal funds rate, the yield curve, and the leading economic indicator (LEI) are used to forecast economic activity a few months from now. So the leading indicators will generally move up (the exception is unemployment insurance claims, which is inverted and will fall) prior to a rise in overall real GDP.

And these indicators will generally fall (because it is inverted, unemployment insurance claims will rise, and the federal funds rate does turn up but lags at the economy's expansions) prior to a fall in overall real GDP.

Where to Find Real GDP

The real GDP numbers are measured every three months. To get an early peek into GDP, check out each quarter's advance measurement. A calendar year's first quarter data generally is released in late April, second quarter in late July, third quarter in late October, and fourth quarter in late January of the following year. Quarterly revisions are released two months after each initial report. Because real GDP measures the country's output, it is big, big news.

National television news and CNNfn report the GDP numbers. Television coverage runs the GDP on the day of its release and for up to a few days following.

Newspaper articles—especially those in national circulation newspapers like the *New York Times*, the *Washington Post*, or *USA Today*—typically run the data for several days after the release of the numbers. It is possible to catch GDP in many regional publications, such as the *Los Angeles Times*, the *Miami Herald*, the *Houston Chronicle*, the *Oregonian*, Louisville's *Courier-Journal*, and the *Chicago Tribune*, as well. Your regional or local newspaper may also cover the GDP story, especially if the quarterly measurements are notable.

If you miss the GDP in the news, you can still easily catch it. The day following its release, check it out in *The Wall Street Journal* (in the Economy section) or *Investor's Business Daily* (in the Business & Economy section).

For instant-news junkies who want just the number, they can phone (202) 602-5306 to retrieve it.

What the Number Says

Real GDP is technically a coincident indicator, meaning that when the economy turns up, real GDP will rise. Likewise, just when the economy falls, real GDP will dip. This makes sense, as GDP is a main gauge that denotes a recession or expansion. As you can see from Chart 3-1, second-quarter 2000 real GDP is roughly $9.3 trillion. As consistent with expansion, you see rising real GDP numbers. Falling real GDP, or even inconsequential rises, suggest the economy is in trouble.

Chart 3-1

Real GDP
Billions of chained* 1996 dollars

	1998	1999	2000
Q1	8,404.9	8,730.0	9,191.8
Q2	8,465.6	8,783.2	9,308.8
Q3	8,537.6	8,905.8	
Q4	8,654.5	9,084.1	

* "Chained" is the term used to indicate that the numbers are calculated to adjust for inflation over two consecutive time periods.

Source: U.S. Department of Commerce Bureau of Economic Analysis

Using GDP

It is vital to look at GDP because it gives us a rough approximation of the economy's business cycles. GDP is a main variable that economists from the National Bureau of Economic Research (NBER) look at when they classify recessions or expansions. It would be easy enough to simply wait to hear from the NBER if we have hit a recession. The problem is that we are already in a recession, or out of a recession, by the time the NBER officially announces it. So by looking at the flow of GDP, we have a rough idea if the economy is in recession or expansion movement.

The pattern of GDP roughly forms the U.S. business cycle. The business cycle has four phases: recession, trough, expansion, and peak. Chart 3-2 illustrates the four phases of the business cycle. Each peak in the cycle is higher than the previous peak because of the long-term growth of the economy.

Chart 3-2, Phases of the Business Cycle

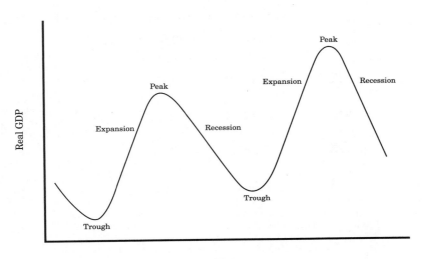

- **Recession:** During the recession phase (shown by a downturn on the chart), economic activity is in a downturn and real GDP will decline. Unemployment is rising and production declining.

- **Trough:** The trough is the lowest point in the cycle. The economy has bottomed out, from which point an upturn will begin.

- **Expansion:** During the expansion phase (shown by an upturn on the chart), economic activity is booming and real GDP will rise. Unemployment is falling and production is rising.

- **Peak:** A peak is reached when economic activity has hit its highest point. After peaking, another recession will occur.

The four phases repeat in an endless succession of highs and lows.

If you are tracking all the leading indicators and they are all falling (except unemployment insurance claims, which are rising), then a fall in real GDP should be right around the corner. See Chart 3-3 for a summary checklist. If the fall in all the indicators is steep, you will likely see a steep fall in real GDP. If the indicators are rising (and claims are falling), the rise in GDP will be here in a matter of a few months.

On the other hand, if you choose to track only one indicator, it would be very wise also to keep abreast of the movements in GDP as an economic benchmark. Just because one economic component has turned in a specific direction does not mean the entire economy will follow suit. You need to track a number of indicators from varying economic sectors before you have a feel for the entire economy.

Chart 3-3

GDP SHIFTS

Indicator	Movement	Expect GDP to
Unemployment Insurance Claims	Rising	Fall
Durable Goods	Falling	Fall
Building Permits	Falling	Fall
S&P 500	Falling	Fall
M2 Money Supply	Falling	Fall
Corporate Profits After Tax	Falling	Fall
Federal Funds Rate	Falling	Fall
Yield Curve	Falling	Fall
Leading Economic Indicator	Falling	Fall

Compilation and Release of GDP

GDP estimates are made quarterly. The BEA releases three estimates according to the following schedule:

Quarter 1: January, February, and March
Advance Estimate: April
Preliminary Estimate: May
Final Estimate: June

Quarter 2: April, May, and June
Advance Estimate: July
Preliminary Estimate: August
Final Estimate: September

Quarter 3: July, August, and September
Advance Estimate: October
Preliminary Estimate: November
Final Estimate: December

Quarter 4: October, November, and December
Advance Estimate: January
Preliminary Estimate: February
Final Estimate: March

The GDP numbers consist of three separate estimates: 1) the advance estimate is published in the first month after the quarter ends; 2) a preliminary estimate follows in the second month; and 3) the final estimate is released in the third month. Each estimate is published at the end of its respective month. More comprehensive data is utilized with each revision.[1] Therefore, as you track the indicators, use the updated GDP figures for an accurate trail of the economy's performance. Note that all the GDP estimates provide impressively reliable indicators of the direction in which economic activity is moving, even though the estimates may vary quite a bit. In a recent study based on sixty quarters of data, each of the three estimates was shown to correctly indicate the direction of the change in economic activity 98 percent of the time.[2]

The BEA also issues the first annual, second annual, and third annual revisions each July when it revises the GDP numbers going back three years. Although not essential for readers, mathematical economists wait for these revisions for precise accuracy in building econometric models.

If You Want to Know More: U.S. Position

The United States is in an enviable position. At more than $9 trillion, the U.S. leads all other industrialized countries in production. Japan follows at over $4 trillion. Next in line, Germany, just exceeds $2 trillion. To top off the winning production figure, the United States experienced stellar growth rates in the 1990s. While a 3 percent rate in GDP is generally considered strong economic growth, over the decade of the '90s the United States consistently outscored this target. Each of the years 1997, 1998, and 1999 produced growth rates in the 4 percent range.

Of course, we are only interested in output due to the real production of more goods and services, not growth in GDP from rising prices. Therefore, the number that you generally hear on the news, and the data in this book, is real GDP. Real GDP has been adjusted to delete any effects of inflation. By looking at how much physical production the country has, and how it is increasing, we can tell just how well the United States is really doing. Real GDP, therefore, measures the material well-being of society, and when it rises, society's very long wish list is further satisfied.

Because the United States is the world's leading industrial country, every quarter, when the GDP figure is released by the BEA, all eyes and ears are open. The figure tells not only those of us in the United States how things are going here, but informs those from other nations as well. Why are people from other countries so interested in U.S. output? Because of our country's lead position in trade and financial markets, U.S. business cycles greatly affect other nations. If the United States is experiencing bad times, we will not be as open to importing goods from other countries. If U.S. production is down, the country's choice of exports to other nations is depressed. In addition, when money becomes scarce in the United States, financial markets tighten, and the world flow of credit is severely dampened. Industrial countries have a tendency to share the broad trends of business cycles, so everyone looks to the leader, the United States.

GDP Versus GNP

Maybe you took a basic economics course in high school and you remember studying about the Gross National Product (GNP), not GDP. What a great memory! And you most likely did study GNP if you took the course prior to 1991. In 1991, the BEA switched from using GNP as the official measure of production to GDP. What is the big difference? GNP measures the output produced by U.S. residents. The catching point: the residents could be in the United States or in another country. GDP, on the other hand, measures production within U.S. borders, whether or not that production is supplied by U.S. residents or nonresidents. Although the differences between the dollar levels of GNP and GDP are minor, the GDP measurement is consistent in coverage with such broad indicators as employment, productivity, and industry output.[3]

Measurement Techniques

Two techniques—expenditure approach and income approach—are available for measuring the total GDP of the economy. The expenditure approach adds the economy's total spending on goods and services. The income approach measures the total income received by individuals as they supply labor, natural resources, capital, and entrepreneurial services in producing the goods and services. Whenever a good or service is produced, someone receives income for producing it. Therefore, these two approaches do provide the same total GDP figure.

The BEA uses both approaches, with the expenditure approach being the most straightforward. So let us look a bit further at total spending in the economy.

It would be next to impossible to add each new purchase—all the new clothes, cars, computers, groceries, and so on—made during the year. The BEA simply calculates the numbers from data collected from various sources, including government and private surveys, censuses, and administrative records.[4]

The sum of all expenditures by consumers, business, government, and the foreign sector make up the expenditure approach to GDP. These four groupings are listed in the GDP accounts as consumption, investment, government, and net exports, respectively.

Every purchase in the economy will fall into one of four categories:

1. **Consumption.** Consumers buy goods and services to increase their well-being. Consumption purchases are divided by the BEA into three categories: i) durable goods, such as furniture, washing machines, and cars; ii) nondurable goods, like clothing, groceries, and paper products; and iii) services, which include visits to the hair stylist, doctor's office, and piano teacher. As you can see from Chart 3-4, consumer purchases propel the economy, representing about two-thirds of all spending in the economy.

2. **Investment.** Investment spending is used to increase capital available to firms and individuals so they can expand businesses or purchase goods. Investment is divided by the BEA into three

categories: i) nonresidential investment, ii) residential investment, and iii) change in business inventories. Nonresidential investment includes spending on such items as industrial buildings, airplanes, and business equipment. Residential investment includes the purchase of mobile homes, single-family homes, and multifamily homes (such as duplexes, condominiums, and apartment buildings). To calculate change in business inventories: if business inventories have risen, the increase is added to GDP. If inventories have fallen, the change is subtracted from GDP.

3. **Government.** Government purchases are divided into federal expenditures and state and local expenditures. Examples of spending items for the federal government include national defense and paying interest on the national debt. State and local governments spend mainly on community services. State expenditures would include such items as education and state highways. Local government expenditures would be items such as public transportation and police protection.

Chart 3-4

Real GDP by Final Expenditure 2000 Q1
(Billions of Chained† 1996 Dollars)

Category	*Dollar Level	Percentage
Consumption	+6,213.5	+68%
Investment	+1,773.6	+19%
Government	+1,565.1	+17%
Net Exports	-376.8	-4%
Total	$9,191.8	

†"Chained" is the term used to indicate that the numbers are calculated to
adjust for inflation over two consecutive time periods.
*Dollar level doesn't sum to total due to rounding discrepancy.
Source: U.S. Department of Commerce Bureau of Economic Analysis

4. **Net Exports.** The last component is net exports. By subtracting all the money the United States spends on imports from what foreigners spend on our exports, we arrive at net exports. The United States tends to import more than we export; therefore, this number is often negative.

Careful Counting

When the BEA calculates GDP, the agency is careful not to count the same output twice. This means that when measuring output, only the cost of the finished product is used. For example, let's assume that you just bought a new leather couch. You probably didn't think of it at the time—you were too excited to get the couch into your den—but the entire selling price was included in GDP. The leather material, cushioning, and wood used to make the couch were not counted when they were sold to the furniture manufacturer. This would have resulted in "double counting"—adding the value of goods and services twice. The value of the leather, cushioning, and wood were taken into account when they became part of your couch. This is why you often hear the term "final value" associated with GDP.

New Production Only

Secondhand, or used, sales are excluded from the total output figure. And there is good reason for doing so. GDP is a measure of the value of final goods and services an economy produces. These goods were counted when they were new—they don't become additional goods by being resold. Assume three years ago you bought a new car for $15,000. At that time, $15,000 of output—your car—was included in GDP. Just last week you sold the car for $9,000 to an acquaintance at work. Good for you, but the total didn't go into GDP because another car was not produced. Resales, or used sales, don't represent new production in the economy; the dollar value is never included in output.

Nonmarket and the Underground Economy

Surely, lots of productive activities occur in your home. Nevertheless, unless you pay for them, they won't show up in GDP. So if you take care of your children, cook, clean, change the oil in your car, and do the laundry, no doubt you are tired, but it won't count as output. Your household chores will not show up in GDP because the activities were not purchased in the marketplace. However, if you hire a cook to prepare your meals, the total amount you pay the cook will show up in GDP. GDP also does not measure unreported transactions or illegal activities. Such activities are referred to as underground activities. Because of the secrecy involved with improper doings, illegal transactions are impossible to tally. Unreported transactions, like hiring someone to mow the lawn or clean your home, are just as difficult to monitor. If you pay an individual more than a base level, the IRS requires the income to be reported and taxed.[5] For individuals who pay "under the table," so to speak (purchases reported by neither buyer nor seller), their transactions are not totaled in GDP.

Although nonmarket and underground activities are not included in GDP, and thus their value is underestimated, GDP consistently measures reported transactions. This track record and stability underscores the point that GDP is indeed a reliable estimate of the economic health of the United States.

What's My GDP Contribution?

When you heard the $9 trillion-plus GDP figure on the news, did you ever dream that you were responsible for part of it? Well, you certainly are. How much? How much do you spend on new goods and services during the year? Since we are talking about the expenditure approach, let's talk about the spending method. It may be rather scary, but just for a moment think about all your purchases over the last year. Your new car, dining room table, television, and ever-increasing grocery store purchases are all part of the total. We are all players in the GDP game.

GDP is massive, it's extensive, and we all propel it through our spending. On the flip side, we can contract GDP through our lack of spending and contribute to a recession.

Feeling guilty? Don't! That is the way of the business cycle. Read on to discover more details about GDP and how its movements parallel the business cycle.

Business Cycle Activity

The material well-being of society is improved by producing more goods and services. Chart 3-5 shows real GDP growth since 1959. As you recall, recessions generally occur when real GDP declines, and booms occur when real GDP expands. So that you may see the depressed GDP trend, the U.S. recessions have been shaded in gray. You can see GDP dip during the last six recessions (the gray bands) and take off once the economy moves out of the recession. And as you can see, the GDP can be a wild and wacky ride!

Chart 3-5

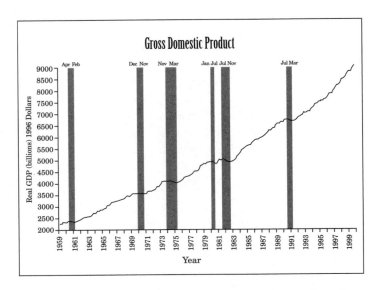

The country has quickly expanded from just under $5 trillion in output to just over $9 trillion in the last twenty years. How much money is $9,000,000,000,000? Output divided among all the people in the United States would result in about $33,000 of production for each man, woman, and child. That is a lot of production. With $9 trillion, we could purchase the entire annual output of Japan, Italy, Canada, Australia, England, Sweden, and Denmark, with a little change to spare.

Dating Business Cycles

The exact dates of recessions and expansions are determined by the Business Cycle Dating Committee of the National Bureau of Economic Research. As you can see from Chart 3-6, recessions are measured from peak to trough (expansions run from the trough to the next peak). Based upon the last five complete cycles the United States has experienced, the average recession has lasted 11.8 months and the average expansion 60.8 months. Therefore, the average business cycle lasts about 72.6 months, or just over six years.[6] The most recent official turning point was March 1991. Sometime during that month, the economy stopped its decline and started surging. In the year 2000, the United States, remarkably, was still experiencing the same expansion period.

Chart 3-6

U.S. Business Cycle Recessions

Reference Dates Peak–Trough	Recession Span	Months of Recession
April 1960– February 1961	April 1960– February 1961	10
December 1969– November 1970	December 1969– November 1970	11
November 1973– March 1975	November 1973– March 1975	16
January 1980– July 1980	January 1980– July 1980	6
July 1981– November 1982	July 1981– November 1982	16
July 1990– March 1991	July 1990– March 1991	8

Before this time, the longest expansion in the entire NBER chronology started in February 1961 and ended in December 1969, a period of 106 months. Sometime through February 2000 the United States experienced an upturn of 107 months, thus surpassing its record. That was great news for our economy. Expansion benefits us all—high employment, strong production, and prosperous times. Nevertheless, history tells us that expansions eventually turn down. Only time will tell. We know from experience that a downturn is on the horizon. The question you will be able to estimate after reading this book is "When?"

Because the NBER wants to determine a turning point as accurately as possible, it does consider additional data along with GDP, such as declines in total income, employment, and trade. And because the NBER looks at other factors, the official turning points will not always coincide with commensurate quarterly shifts in real GDP. But still, it's a great reflection of business cycles.

The committee last met in 1992 to determine the date of the trough in early 1991.[7] When the GDP numbers soften, you can bet the group will keep a watchful eye.

Summary

The leading indicators reported in this book all foretell economic downturns and upturns in the economy. And although the business cycle is composed of movements based upon several other factors, fluctuations in real GDP are at the heart of the cycle. We therefore use GDP as a proxy for movements in the overall business cycle. So, in other words, when the indicators peak and start a downward progression, you will likely see a fall in real GDP right around the corner. When the indicators hit bottom and start an upward trail, real GDP will soon be picking up. The following real GDP tracking chart and the summary chart in chapter 13 provide spaces for the advance, preliminary, and final real GDP figures so that you can monitor the economy's overall fluctuations. If you are tracking GDP, you are more likely to know if we have entered a recession or expansion before it has officially been announced.

Tracking Gross Domestic Product (GDP)

Watch real GDP to monitor the size and strength of the economy or if you want verification on the general direction of the economy. You will know if the country has entered a recession or expansion before you hear the official announcement.

Frequency: The indicator is released on a quarterly basis.

When: The advance estimate is published late in the first month after the quarter ends. Two revisions follow—a preliminary estimate follows late in the second month, and the final estimate is released late in the third month.

Where: Television coverage runs the day of the GDP's release and for up to a few days following. Newspaper stories typically run for up to a few days after the release of the numbers. For the numbers, see a national circulation newspaper such as the *New York Times,* the *Washington Post,* or *USA Today,* which frequently covers GDP and especially when the number is pivotal to upcoming Federal Reserve actions.

Alternatively, you can obtain the figure from many regional publications such as the *Los Angeles Times,* the *Miami Herald,* the *Houston Chronicle,* the *Oregonian,* Louisville's *Courier-Journal,* and the *Chicago Tribune.* Many other regional newspapers cover the GDP story if the quarterly measurements are notable. If you miss the number in the news, another easy way to get the number is to look in *The Wall Street Journal* (in the Economy section) or *Investor's Business Daily* (in the Business & Economy section) on the day following its release. You can also call (202) 602-5306 to retrieve the number.

How: The press and television news generally will report the quarterly real GDP number expressed as a seasonally adjusted annual rate (such as $9,308.8 billion), the percentage change for the respective quarter (such as "first quarter real GDP increased 4.8 percent"), or both. A 3 percent rate in GDP growth is typically considered healthy because a lower number suggests a slowing economy and higher numbers suggest stellar growth.

Use the following chart to track GDP.

GDP

Year:	
Q1: Jan/Feb/Mar	
Q2: Apr/May/Jun	
Q3: Jul/Aug/Sep	
Q4: Oct/Nov/Dec	

Notes on Trend:

Chapter 4

A Good Time to Job Hunt?
Unemployment Insurance Claims

"Employment is nature's physician, and is essential to human happiness."

—Galen

Your job is probably one of the most important parts of your life. It affects your lifestyle, self-esteem, and your pocketbook. And your job clearly is affected by what's going on in the economy. Even though it is how you spend the majority of your waking hours, your job boils down to the sale of your skills to a buyer (your employer) at a price set by the marketplace. When the economy is down, it becomes much more difficult for your employer to purchase your skills. In tough economic times, you are much more likely to lose your job, unless you are employed in a sector that will still hire even when the economy goes bad. Hospitals, computer technology firms, nursing homes, and grocery stores are all examples of businesses that provide services or goods that are always in demand, even in downtimes and, consequently, continue to hire employees even in the throes of a recession. Conversely, when the economy is booming and employment is strong, companies are willing to pay top dollar for your skills. A strong economy is a good environment in which to negotiate better pay, working conditions, and benefits. A career in a luxury-related business (such as a luxury-car dealership, cruise line, hotel chain, jewelry store, or upscale clothing store) skyrockets during expansions, but contracts during a downturn.

The economic indicator that you will want to watch for all job-related decisions is the unemployment insurance claims indicator. Track this indicator on an ongoing basis so that when job-related issues arise for you, you will be able to see the indicator's trends and know when to make an employment move and/or what your negotiating strength is at any given time. The unemployment insurance claims indicator will be useful to you whether you are thinking about quitting your job and going back to school, changing careers, or asking for a raise. This one economic indicator can help you maximize your career plans.

Where to Find Unemployment Insurance Claims

The unemployment claims number is easy to find. It is commonly referred to as "new jobless claims," "weekly jobless claims," or "initial claims" in the popular press. The claims numbers are released every Thursday morning and receive prominent coverage on Thursdays and Fridays on national television news; in addition, CNNfn covers this indicator. It is generally reported in Friday's editions of newspapers carrying the release. Big papers like the *New York Times* and the *Washington Post* routinely publish the number. You can also oftentimes catch it in regional publications like the *Houston Chronicle,* the *Los Angeles Times,* the *Chicago Tribune,* the *Miami Herald,* and Louisville's *Courier-Journal.* Other regional and local newspapers cover the indicator as news merits.

If you miss it in the news, catch the number in Friday's editions of *The Wall Street Journal* (in the Economy section) and *Investor's Business Daily* (in the Economic Briefs section). Or, for a summary of the new claims numbers for the last two weeks, you can call the recorded message at (202) 693-3231.

To plan your job-related decisions, it is recommended that you check the numbers for three months, at least a couple of times a month, to get a feel for the trend.

What the Number Says

What is the first thing people do when they suddenly find themselves without a job? You guessed it. They make a quick dash to the unemployment office to file for unemployment insurance. The total number of new claims filed at all of the state unemployment agencies for the week is exactly the statistic we are interested in. When the nation is coming upon hard economic times, people begin to lose their jobs, and you will see the number of claims rise. On average, the upward trend of claims actually starts about one year before a recession hits. So, by simply viewing this number, you have significant advance warning to plan your job strategy. Claims continue to rise steadily during a recession.

Historically, about eight weeks before the economy picks up again, the number of claims will start to fall. People are called back to work as companies start to expand production. There will be less traffic at the state unemployment insurance office. As the economy continues to prosper, the number of unemployment claims falls even further.

Unemployment insurance claims is such a good leader of the economy, it is one of the ten component indicators included in the Leading Economic Indicator (LEI). And claims are easy to interpret. Unlike all the other indicators we are using, when claims rise, it is a bad thing. Companies are letting people go; it will be tough to find a new job. People are hoping they are not the ones to get a pink slip. And contrary to the other indicators, when claims are falling, the economy is booming. It is a great time to make a job switch or look for advancement. So let's see just how this topsy-turvy indicator can work for you.

Using Unemployment Insurance Claims

By monitoring the number of unemployment insurance claims, you can easily gauge your career options. Should you quit your job and go back to school? Suppose you hear on the nightly news that the number of unemployment insurance claims has been on a steady rise for eleven weeks in a row. Are you going to lose your job? Not necessarily, but you do have some cause for concern. If your responsibilities are essential to the running of the company, you may be somewhat secure. But if you are in a less vital department, you definitely have some worries. So if you have been thinking about going back to school, now is a good time to make the move. Claims rise for roughly one whole year before the recession actually hits. When the recession strikes, the layoffs will really swell, so if you spot the trend early, you have a number of months to plan your exit to college.

Is it a good time to approach the boss for a raise? A high quality performance is the main factor in a salary hike. If your performance ratings have been strong, then don't hesitate to knock on the boss' door. But you must wait for the best time. You may be a fantastic employee, but if you ask for a raise in the middle of a slump, you will get turned down cold. The ideal time to knock on your boss' door is when you notice that the number of filed claims has been on the decline for some months. The country will be in the early stages of an expansion. Business is booming and so are your company's profits. The powers that be are going to be much more inclined now to let you share in the company's wealth. Remember too, when claims are low, the employment picture is strong. The company doesn't want to lose you because it knows it may have real trouble replacing you. It is likely going to do whatever it takes to keep you happy. So have your performance ratings in hand, wait for the right time, and go get that raise.

Looking to get back into the job market? Knowing the level of unemployment insurance claims can help you plan your job search strategy. Suppose you discover that unemployment claims are notably high. Don't stress. It is not going to be impossible to land a job, it is just going to take a bit more work. The country is in a depressed period and the competition for jobs is going to be tough. You are going to have to be more diligent than the next guy. So stop by businesses, fill out applications, and make that important face-to-face contact. Talk to friends, relatives, and acquaintances to look for leads. Try the mainstay recession-proof businesses before the competition does. Be sure to read the wants ads in the newspaper to see what types of companies are hiring in your area. You will be able to compose a list of companies that will be hiring even at the height of a recession. It may be the local supermarket, movie theater, or pharmacy. The key is to find businesses that provide services or goods that people will always pay for, even though times are tough. If, however, unemployment claims are at the low end of the spectrum, you have some vital information and a bit of bargaining power. It is hard to find good employees when employment is so strong. Employers will welcome hardworking people like you. So try a place where you would really like to work and request a good work schedule. You now can be a bit choosier.

Ready for a new job? At some time in our lives, most of us will change jobs. Maybe you are interested in a different job because it will pay more. Or maybe you are interested in shifting to a new field that is more exciting and interesting. Whatever your motives, timing is the key. You recall that, on average, claims begin to fall eight weeks before an expansion begins. So if you've been watching claims fall for several months, that is a fantastic time to make a job switch. The country has had some time to feel the beneficial effects of the expansion. Businesses feel more comfortable hiring more employees as they open new stores, expand production, and build facilities. You can have confidence that your new employer won't be laying you off in such a prosperous environment. Go with a company that interests you because business is booming universally. But for an added bang, take a look at luxury-related businesses. Frill purchases really soar during expansionary phases. Feeling prosperous, people spend money more freely on luxuries like boats, designer clothes, fancy cars, and jewelry. They also spend a great deal more on travel—staying at nice hotels and taking great cruises. Fine dining at elegant restaurants is also big business when times are good. So the boat shops, upscale clothing stores, high-end auto dealerships, jewelry emporiums, nice hotel chains, cruise lines, and fine dining establishments to name just a few, will need employees desperately. Luxury businesses will offer you first-class employment packages to entice you away from other companies. So if claims are low, don't jump at the first job offer. Plan your strategy, negotiate, and deal yourself a top-notch job. However, anytime you notice a potential upward trend in claims, and you have a stable work environment, it's best to stay put until you notice a definite pattern. A recession may be on the horizon, a factor you will want to consider before undertaking a job search.

Considering part-time work? Or maybe you are just entering the workforce and want to start with short hours. If you are interested in part-time work, take a hint from the numbers. Businesses hire a great number of part-time employees when the economy is down. So if you see the number of claims start to briskly rise or if claims are already elevated, you have abundant opportunities. Firms can get through depressed times by replacing full-time employees with part-timers. Not only is it cheaper to employ a part-time person (who works fewer hours and generally doesn't receive benefits), but in a depressed economy firms often don't have the workload to justify retaining a full-time employee. So when full-timers are filing for unemployment claims, part-timers get ready to move into the workforce.

There are many other scenarios: teachers looking for summer jobs, those set on career advancement, people looking to cut back their hours, or individuals considering a second job. The job decisions are many and complex. But the decisions don't have to be difficult. Let the unemployment insurance claims indicator be your guide. Regardless of your job decision, you must ask yourself one simple question when you read the weekly claims report: Is the trend up or down? If the trend in claims is up, it is more difficult to find a job, raises and advancement are not likely, release notices will be plentiful, but recession-proof businesses will still be hiring. If the trend in claims is down, employment opportunities are strong, raises and advances are likely, attractive job packages (benefits, great hours, and paid vacation) are plentiful, and luxury-related businesses are really booming.

Compilation and Release of the Number

Anybody can file for unemployment insurance, but all the claims won't be granted. Still, the initial filed number gives us the best early peek at the employment outlook, even displaying better leading ability than the widely referenced unemployment rate.[1] People who leave a job without good cause, choose to retire, or are dismissed because of misconduct ultimately won't receive any benefits.

The popular press does not report the actual number of new claims. The number the press routinely reports as "new jobless claims" is actually seasonally adjusted. It is common practice for economic indicators to be seasonally adjusted because many numbers show seasonal movement that repeats every year. For example, construction work drops off every year in the winter months and there is always big pre-Christmas employment. Such seasonal influences have been removed to aid in interpreting trends.

In addition, the press oftentimes reports the "four-week average." The four-week seasonally adjusted moving average has the most stable track record because it smoothes out the trend of the weekly figures.[2] Simply put, the claims number is an average of values taken from four surrounding weekly periods.

The four-week average of claims is more level over time. It doesn't bounce around quite as much, but either number viewed over the long-term will do the trick. To be certain that you are tracking the upward or downward movement in claims, be sure you are looking at the same statistic each week.

Here is how *The Wall Street Journal* reported on the weekly claims numbers released on July 27, 2000:

[T]he number of Americans filing new claims for jobless benefits fell a larger-than-expected 40,000 last week to 272,000, the lowest level since mid-April. The Labor Department said that the four-week average of new claims, considered a better gauge because it smoothes out fluctuations, dropped to 299,250 claims from 308,000 in the previous week.[3]

Let's look at claims for the four-week average, since *The Wall Street Journal* reports the number. Reflect, for a moment, on what the number really means. A total of 299,250 new unemployment claims were filed throughout the United States that week. This is a staggering statistic. No wonder state unemployment claims alone have reached almost $19 billion a year. Yet, comparatively speaking, unemployment claims are quite low, which as you recall is a good thing. This data is consistent with a strong expansion. The downward trend in claims began just weeks before the expansion began in April 1991. Although it has moderated since the early phase of the expansion, claims are still exhibiting a downward trend. Further stressing the trend is a 8,750 drop in claims from the previous week.

Remember, when you see the number of claims each week, look for a significant and sustained upward or downward trend. We now know that in an expansion, claims fall. The drop-off will be more marked and significant at the early part of the expansion. But the number of claims will continue to decline throughout the prosperous period. You may have weeks in an expansion when the number of claims will stay fixed or will rise. For example, in the early part of the December 1982–June 1990 expansion, claims showed a sharp downward trend. The first adjusted claims report issued in December and subsequent reports illustrate the occasional bumpy downward pattern: 557,000; 533,000; 516,000; 489,000; 534,000; 510,000; 479,000.[4]

Did the one jolt upward mean the country was about to enter another recession? Certainly not, it was just a normal weekly fluctuation in the claims numbers. You begin to suspect a recession only when the number of claims has hit a low point and starts a sustained movement upward. When you hit a recession you know that claims will largely rise each week. Yet, you will have weeks when the number stays constant or falls. As an illustration, at the onset of the July 1990–March 1991 recession, claims moved predominantly upward. The weekly numbers, beginning with the first report that July, show a chiefly upward pattern, with the exception of one stationary period: 358,000; 360,000; 366,000; 366,000; 379,000; 383,000; 397,000.[5]

So before you share predictions of imminent recovery or doom, look for an overriding trend in the weekly movement of claims. And as with all indicators, complement your viewing of the numbers with good solid common sense.

If You Want to Know More: Employment and Training Administration

The unemployment claims numbers are published each week by the Employment and Training Administration (ETA) of the Division of Labor. Along with providing data for the Unemployment Insurance Weekly Claims Report, the ETA gives grants to states to deliver job training, employment services, labor market information, and income maintenance services. The ETA works closely with state and local work-force development systems.[6]

Each Thursday at 8:30 A.M. Eastern Time, the new unemployment figures are released. The released numbers are for the previous week, ending Saturday. So this means there are only five days of lag time. With each release, the prior week's published figures are revised. But for our tracking purposes, it is not essential to note these minor updates. Annual revisions to the numbers are made in January and released in February each year.

Eligibility for Unemployment Benefits

Now, if one does receive the benefits, it will usually be about half the amount earned while employed, up to your state's maximum benefit amount. The average weekly benefit runs just over $200 nationwide. In most states, benefits may be received for a maximum of twenty-six weeks. During periods of high unemployment, additional weeks of benefits may become available. When extended benefits are granted, recipients are not included in the state's claims numbers. To be eligible to receive claims, in most states:

1. You must meet the state requirements for wages earned or time worked during a one-year period prior to the claim.

2. You must have become unemployed (or had your working hours reduced) through no fault of your own.

3. You must be able to work: this means that you are physically and mentally capable of working every day of the week for which you are claiming benefits.

4. You must be available for work: this means you are ready to start a job immediately. It also means you have transportation and do not have to remain at home to care for children or other dependents. You must be available for work every day of the week for which you are claiming benefits.

5. You must actively seek work: this means that for each week of benefits you claim, you must make an active search for work and do all that is reasonable to secure employment.[7]

A recipient does not automatically remain eligible for unemployment benefits. Among the requirements to maintain benefits, claimants must keep all scheduled appointments at local unemployment insurance offices and must continue to meet the previously noted eligibility requirements. Further, if a suitable job is offered to a recipient, the individual must accept it, or risk losing the unemployment benefits.

Financing Unemployment Insurance

Are you curious who actually pays for unemployment insurance? Chiefly, the insurance system is financed by a payroll tax that employers legally must fund. However, a few states do require a small contribution from employees. And does it ever add up quickly. Nearly eight million people received $20.6 billion in benefits (under regular and special programs) in fiscal year 1997. During the same period, approximately 6.3 million employers paid state unemployment compensation taxes of a whopping $22.2 billion.[8]

Some Unemployment Exists in a Strong Economy

Economists expect some types of unemployment to exist even during a strong economy. Most economists define full employment at 94 percent. The second most common definition places full employment at 95 percent. When the economy is strong, therefore, roughly 5 to 6 percent unemployment will remain. While there is a minor debate in the economics field on the actual number that defines full employment, there is no controversy on the two types of unemployment—frictional and structural—that still exist in a fully employed economy. So let us examine further the types of unemployment that exist even when the economy is prospering.

Frictional unemployment accounts for individuals between jobs, job discharges, those reentering the workforce, and those just entering the labor force. This group includes people who leave a position because they want a better job or because they are moving to a different area. In the working world, employers routinely dismiss employees, and this falls in the area of frictional unemployment. The frictionally unemployed include young people just out of high school or college who are entering the working world for the first time. Individuals may be reentering for a number of reasons, such as a parent who has taken time off to raise children or a recently divorced spouse who must jump back into the working world for financial reasons. The frictionally unemployed category is not of much concern to society because it arises from the normal operation, or flux, of the labor market. Economist Steve Slavin estimates that at any given time, 2 or 3 percent of the labor force is frictionally unemployed.[9]

Structural unemployment occurs when the unemployed don't have the necessary qualifications and skills for available jobs. Due to the rapidly changing technological environment in which we live, structural unemployment has become more of a dilemma in recent years. Job training programs, such as those offered by state unemployment offices, can help ease this problem.

You can get a feel for structural unemployment by viewing the help wanted ads in the local newspaper. Though the United States has very low unemployment now, most likely your newspaper is full of want ads. You likely will find many positions available in the computer, technology, and engineering areas. These are the major areas where the country is structurally unemployed. There are not enough people with skills in these technical fields, and it is a nationwide problem. Slavin notes that another 2 to 3 percent of the labor force is structurally unemployed.[10]

So, though the country is at full employment, unemployment claims will still exist, largely due to frictional and structural unemployment. Society expects frictional and structural unemployment. Job shifting and changing industry patterns make the two types of unemployment inevitable. Cyclical unemployment, on the other hand, causes great distress to our society as a whole. Herein lies the main problem for our economy. Economists refer to any rate of unemployment above the 5 to 6 percent level as cyclical unemployment. There are simply more unemployed individuals than available jobs. Cyclical unemployment occurs when the economy slows. Any time this happens, not only will economic growth of the country suffer, but the cyclically unemployed will suffer as well. They can experience loss of self-esteem, depression, and despair. In short, cyclical unemployment leads to trouble.

During the recession in 1982, for example, when the annual unemployment rate reached 9.7 percent, frictional and structural unemployment accounted for roughly 5 to 6 percent of the total. The remaining 3.7 to 4.7 percent was categorized as cyclical unemployment. From 1999 to 2000, cyclical unemployment was essentially nonexistent and the United States was experiencing the prosperity of being fully employed.

In 1999 the unemployment rate for the United States was 4.2 percent. Iowa had the lowest unemployment at 2.5 percent while West Virginia's was the highest at 6.6 percent.

Business Cycle Activity

As you can see from Chart 4-1, claims for unemployment insurance hit bottom many months before a recession and rise during the recession, because people need unemployment insurance during tough times. The series peaks and starts to fall just weeks before the economy starts to expand.

Chart 4-1

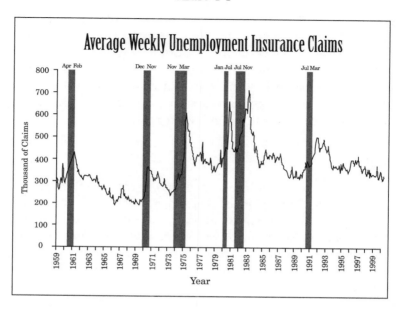

A sharp increase in the number of filed claims should alert you to potential bad times for the economy, while a pattern of marked declines suggests prosperous economic times.

Financial Participants' Reaction

A great plus to this labor market indicator is its frequent and timely release. Its timeliness has made it a long-term favorite of the financial markets. It is easy to see why this unemployment claims number is a financial favorite. Markets like quick and current data. There is only five days lag time in the data, and claims are released every Thursday. If the number is unusually high or low, both the bond and stock markets will respond dramatically. This one number can influence the trend of the market the entire day of its release.

The bond market generally reacts favorably to high claims. High unemployment, particularly with minuscule inflationary pressures, suggests lower interest rates are on the horizon. If you are a bond holder, this is positive news. Your old bond pays a higher interest rate than new bonds just coming to market, so the value of your old bond will increase.

The stock market's reaction is much harder to predict. Stock players will probably react favorably to a moderate increase in initial claims. An increase in new unemployment claims indicates slowing economic growth. If inflation is low, and no interest rate increases are expected by the Federal Reserve, market participants may count on lower interest rates. The accompanying lower interest rates are generally good for borrowing costs, so stock prices will rise. But if new claims are high, stock market concern over the depressed economy may override the positive benefit of lower rates, resulting in low stock prices.

Summary

The labor market is the mover and shaker of the U.S. economy. For a peek at the trend of employment conditions, study new claims for unemployment insurance. The weekly indicator of initial claims provides constant updates and feedback on employment conditions. The financial markets, therefore, examine it closely.

You too, should look at it closely. Don't make a career move before checking in on the claims indicator. When claims start to rise, you have some important information about the job outlook. The average advance recession warning is about one year. Once the recession hits, the layoffs will skyrocket. Use the time to plan wisely. Think again about leaving your stable employment situation. It would be wise to wait until a better time. If you are thinking about going back to college or to graduate school, it is a good time to make the move. There is good news for part-timers, who have boundless opportunities in a depressed economy.

When claims start to trend downward, the average expansion warning is eight weeks. The economy will soon prosper and the employment picture will strengthen even further. Employers will have difficulty finding and retaining good employees. Use the information to your advantage to negotiate a raise, feel confident making that job switch, or secure your dream job.

Thinking about a career move? The number of new claims filed at the state unemployment insurance offices will advise you.

Tracking Unemployment Insurance Claims

Check out the unemployment claims number for guidance about job-related decisions.

Frequency: The indicator is released on a weekly basis. Check the numbers for three months to get a feel for the trend.

When: The claims are released every Thursday morning.

Where: The number receives prominent coverage on Thursdays and Fridays on national television news; CNNfn also covers this indicator. If you miss the release on television, catch it in the Friday edition of *The Wall Street Journal* (in the Economy section) or *Investor's Business Daily* (in the Economic Briefs section). Generally, it is reported in Friday editions of papers carrying the story. Big papers such as the *New York Times* and the *Washington Post* routinely carry the number. You can catch it in regional publications such as the *Houston Chronicle*, the *Los Angeles Times*, the *Chicago Tribune*, the *Miami Herald*, and Louisville's *Courier-Journal*. Other papers cover the indicator as news merits. Or for a summary of claims for the last two weeks, you can call a recorded message at (202) 693-3231.

How: The data is released as a whole number such as 272,500. Look for commentary on the numbers such as "signal of a tight labor market and slowdown in the economy" or "sign of an easing labor market and rebound in the economy."

Use the following chart to track unemployment insurance claims:

Unemployment Insurance Claims

January	
February	
March	
April	
May	
June	
July	
August	
September	
October	
November	
December	

Notes on Trend:

Chapter 5

Bargain Shopping?
Durable Goods Orders

"When you buy, use your eyes and your mind, not your ears."
—Czech proverb

Durable goods are big-ticket items with an expected life of one year or more, such as cars, furniture, computers, electronics, home appliances, medical supplies, and aircraft. These represent the infrequent but high-cost purchases that you'll need to make at different points in your life and those purchases that you may need to finance if you haven't been saving up for them. Durable goods orders represent commitments to pay for orders placed with domestic manufacturers. The number measures the dollar amount of orders received by U.S. manufacturers from both U.S. and foreign customers.

Durable goods orders provide keen insight into manufacturing activity and consequently the overall health of the economy. When orders rise, manufacturing will pick up, and so will the economy. New manufacturing is a substantial mover of our economy—orders for durable goods represent roughly $250 billion each month. And when factories suffer a decline in orders, it is a bad sign for the entire economy. Production lines halt, which cripples economic performance.

So to be prepared to make a decision about buying a new car, piece of furniture, photography equipment, big screen television, or appliance such as a washer, dryer, dishwasher, or refrigerator, watch the durable goods indicator. Because when supply increases, prices will fall. And on most consumer durable purchases, shopping during an expansion provides a very competitive atmosphere and the bargains are hot. But you needn't stay away from the stores completely if you want to find a deal in a recessionary period. If you need to finance your durable purchase, the low interest rates will be a perk. And when the economy is down, luxury demand tumbles, so prices fall as well.

Computer and other technology prices are somewhat different from other durable goods in that engineering advances cause prices to fall every time a new generation is released. Technology items, therefore, react less to shifts in the economy and more to technology advances.

Where to Find Durable Goods Orders

The advance report on durable goods orders is released each month to the press early in the morning, roughly three weeks from the end of the data month. It is released along with a revision of the previous month, which you should jot down because the revisions are often significant. Because the durable goods indicator is a bond and stock market favorite, it is widely reported by national television news on the day of its release and the day following. CNNfn routinely covers the durable numbers. It generally runs the day following the release in many newspapers, including the *Washington Post*, the *New York Times*, and *USA Today*, which are all widely available. You may also find coverage in Louisville's *Courier-Journal*, the *Houston Chronicle*, the *Los Angeles Times*, the *Chicago Tribune*, the *Miami Herald*, and the *Oregonian*. Other regional and local newspapers cover the number as news merits.

If you miss the number on the news, it is covered in *The Wall Street Journal* (in the Economy section) and *Investor's Business Daily* (in the Business & Economy section) on the day following its release.

For planning your big-ticket purchases, check this indicator for at least three months in order to get a feel for the trend.

What the Number Says

New orders are an important indicator of future economic activity because they provide a hint of upcoming manufacturing activity and future business trends. The more orders a manufacturer receives, the more inclined it is to increase production. On the flip side, if new orders fall, producers will plan to decrease production so inventories don't stack up. Major category industry groupings in durable goods include lumber and wood products; furniture and fixtures; stone, clay, and glass products; primary metal industries, fabricated metal products, industrial machinery and equipment, electronic and other electrical equipment, transportation equipment, and other durable goods.[1] So the types of durable orders are vast. This number includes orders for intermediate goods such as glass, iron, wood, and electronic components used to produce other durable goods. It also includes orders for finished industrial items such as office, construction, and farm equipment. The dollar value of transportation goods such as ships, tanks, and aircraft is huge. And, of course, it includes the durables mentioned above, those goods consumers regularly purchase such as fans, video equipment, CD players, dishwashers, televisions, and much more. It's all packed into one number. The durable goods number is one quick look into the entire durable manufacturing sector.

Durable goods orders is a leading indicator for both recessions and expansions. A recession is on the way roughly ten months after durables peak and start to fall. Indications that the economy is entering an expansion period is more immediate; durables will hit bottom and start to rise just one month prior to the economy rebounding.

So, when durables start a noticeable downward trend, manufacturing will slow, and trouble for the economy is just around the corner. The major consumer durables industries like electronics, appliances, furniture, computer technology, and the automotive sector are highly competitive. If you are a great shopper, you can always find a bargain, but if you are looking for widespread deals, a recession is not going to be the best time to shop. During a recession, we see an enormous reduction in the dollar volume of durable orders. Consequently, the supply of durable goods falls as well. Individuals aren't buying. When manufacturers reduce supply, prices will rise.

Conversely, when orders hit bottom and start moving up, the expansion is just around the corner—one month on average. A sharp increase in the dollar volume of consumer durables, hence supply, will lower prices. These industries tend to be highly competitive and operate on thin profit margins.[2] These businesses make their money by selling large volume at low prices—something they can do easily in an expansion and still come out ahead. Just think back to the last time you got a deal on a household appliance. Most likely, it wasn't during a downtime in the economy. If you bought a washer, dryer, vacuum cleaner, trash compactor, oven, or freezer in the last ten years when orders were high, you probably found yourself a bargain.

Using Durable Goods

By watching the total durable goods orders every month, you can get a handle on the level of orders. The factories supply the stores, so by watching this one number you can time your bargain shopping.

We have all been there. Your household appliance—refrigerator, oven, microwave, dishwasher, water heater, garbage disposal, washer, or dryer—is just about to give out. Appliances are expensive but necessary. This is a purchase you are going to have to make regardless of what's going on in the economy. But durables can still provide some shopping hints for these costly items. If your appliance has managed to break down when durables orders are high, you are lucky. Consumer durables are going to be up in supply, there is a wide selection, and price will be competitive. But watch out. If you need to finance, the interest rate won't be low. Just one month after durables orders rise, the expansion hits. And along with all the competition for funds comes an increased interest rate. Rates will likely hit a high point at the height of the expansion. So if you need to make a durable goods purchase during the early part of the durables rise, you can benefit from the increased supply and bargain prices, and still find some good interest rates. Your first try for a loan should always be your local bank, credit union, or savings bank. Such institutional lenders often offer better rates than the retailer or manufacturer. This is particularly true if you already have an established relationship with the financial institution. On the other hand, if you are buying when durables are down, you may not find a great competitive sale, but you can find a great low interest rate (rates fall during recession periods).

Planning on buying new furniture? Look to durables. Just as with any high-priced purchase, you'll want to do your homework and price furniture at several different stores. When durables orders start an upward shift you know that production lines will start moving to fill those orders. Stores will soon be stocked with a complete selection. And along with an increased selection comes a fantastic competitive price, and you may also have some negotiating clout for items that are highly competitive. But if you hear on the business news that orders for durables goods have taken a sharp downturn, you know that manufacturing and store selection is going to be down very, very soon. Even if this downturn is not a sustained fall which precedes a recession, a drop in orders will likely temporarily cause selection to be down. If you really want that new furniture, go for it before the selection is reduced.

What about a technology purchase? Technology purchases are wide and varied: television sets, computers, video players, and CD players, to name just a few. Most of us are intrigued by the advances in technology over the last few decades. Engineers are constantly working on better and more efficient ways to make these products. Technological advances allow workers to make more—and better—products at a lower cost. Such advances alone, regardless of economic activity, increase supply and reduce price. If you read in the newspaper that durable goods have been on the rise for four months, you know the store shelves will soon be jam-packed full of selections. But the news is even better for products heavily affected by technology. This is why you can go to the store and see the price of a computer drop significantly over a matter of weeks. Part of the reduction is attributable to the booming economy, but another part is due to the technological advances that lower price. Consequently, for a technology purchase, your best deals come when durables are high and competition is fierce. However, even when durables drop and recession hits, you will still see prices fall (although not as significantly) due to technology advances. So if you are high tech, feel confident about buying such items any time in the economy. If you are not in a hurry to buy, go to the store every week and check prices on these items—prices are likely to just keep dropping.

When can you get the best deal on a car? When the country is in an expansion, expect to pay more for car makes and models that are in demand and less for the slower movers. Cars that are considered luxury vehicles are in high demand when an expansion hits. People have money in a boom period and can afford the "hot" luxury cars. Find a basic car make and model that is not moving, and the car dealer probably will give you a great deal just to move it off the lot. Often the top-line car dealers get full sticker price and have a full waiting list for interested buyers. Suppose that you read in the newspaper that durables are picking up and you suspect that the country is coming off a recession. If you are going to make a luxury car purchase, run to the dealership while supply is high and demand has not yet kicked in. Once the expansion is in full swing, supply may be rising but demand outpaces the supply, and prices may skyrocket. (That is why it's not unheard of for dealers to occasionally get more than the sticker price on hot cars.)

> When durables are high, if you want a great deal, buy basic. But when durables are low, the luxury market slides, so you can buy luxury at a great price.

If durable goods are on the rise and you are in the market for a durable, be sure to save your receipt and continue checking prices for a few weeks once you have made your purchase. If your item goes on sale, most stores will reimburse you if you return in a matter of weeks and present your receipt.

Maybe you read in the newspaper that durables have remained low over the last few years and there are no signs of recovery. It is not the best time to be buying a big-ticket item because supply is low, times are tough, and deals are not plentiful. If you're in a tight spot and must purchase at this time, ask if you can purchase the store's floor model. Many stores sell them at deep discounts.

So before you go to the store, take a hint from durable goods orders. Generally, when durables orders are up there will soon be more supply. Increased supply brings reduced price. When durables are down, the store selection will be too. So don't spend too much time at the mall. There will be better times for sale shopping.

Compilation and Release of the Number

The durable goods figure largely includes orders received and filled during the respective month, plus orders received for future delivery. The number also includes the effect of contract changes, cancellations, and adjustments on earlier reported orders. Orders include legally supported binding documents such as signed contracts, letters of award, or letters of intent. There are exceptions because orders in some industries do not fall under this definition.[3]

Not all firms will report new orders, and some exclude new orders received for specific products shipped from inventory. Therefore, because the tally information for new orders is incomplete, an estimate of new orders suffices nicely. The estimate of new orders is calculated from the following basic formula, which includes the effects of cancellations and modifications of previously reported orders:

Current Month's Estimate of Shipments
+ Current Month's Unfilled Orders
− Prior Month's Unfilled Orders
= New Orders

The estimate therefore includes orders that are received and filled in the same month, along with orders not yet filled.

New orders for durable goods are reported in both seasonally adjusted and non–seasonally adjusted data.[4] These numbers are reported in current dollars and are not adjusted for inflation. You want to view the seasonally adjusted data because it is an average. And it is easy to find because that is the number reported by the media. Don't make quick judgments about downturns or upturns. The monthly shifts can be fairly significant, so this indicator should be used with care. Look at the monthly changes over a long time frame.

Following is the full press release on new orders for the advance report for June 2000 data, released to the press on July 27, 2000:

> New orders for manufactured durable goods in June increased $22.1 billion or 10.0 percent to $243.2 billion, the Department of Commerce, Bureau of Census reported today. This follows a 7.0 percent May increase and is the largest increase since July 1991. Excluding transportation, new orders increased 0.8 percent. Year-to-date, new orders are 11.1 percent above the same period a year ago; new orders for the second quarter are 4.3 percent above the first quarter.
>
> Transportation equipment had the largest increase, $20.8 billion or 43.0 percent to $69.1 billion, mostly due to aircraft and parts. This is the largest increase on record. Industrial machinery and equipment increased $0.6 billion or 1.3 percent to $44.1 billion. Primary metals increased $0.3 billion or 1.6 percent to $16.1 billion. Electronic and other electrical equipment, up four of the last five months, increased $0.1 billion or 0.3 percent to $47.1 billion.[5]

Generally, the press reports on the total number of durable goods, durables excluding transportation, and any other segment change that was notable. Although in the above-reported month a chunk of the increase was from transportation, all of the other major categories showed moderate rises as well. This report is certainly strong support of the upward rise in durable orders that you see in expansionary times. Let's look at the flip side—when durables start to plummet.

Remember that on average, the economy enters a recession ten months after durable goods peak and start to plummet. The last official recession in the United States began in July 1990 (and ran through March 1991). Durables peaked four months prior to the recession, and then began its somewhat bumpy downward fall. At that time, if you were trying to pinpoint a recession, there were plenty of signs of weakness in the economy. Take a look at *The Wall Street Journal* story below on the June 1990 data (just one month before the official designation of a recession), which showed a major drop in virtually every durable goods category (a big red flag):

NEW GOVERNMENT STATISTICS SHOW LINGERING WEAKNESS
IN THE MANUFACTURING SECTOR

Orders to factories for durable goods dropped 3.2 percent in June after a 4.2 percent rise in May, the Commerce Department reported. Nearly every category of the big-ticket items suffered declines: transportation equipment, primary metals, machinery, and military equipment...

"I think these numbers say the improvement has gone as far as it can go," said Robert McGee, an economist at Tokai Bank in New York...

Last month's decline brought new orders to $124.69 billion in June. For the first six months of the year, new orders came to $744.7 billion, 1.5% below a year earlier.[6]

Because this is a volatile number, you really have to watch it for some time to recognize an upward or downward shift. Read the newspaper analyses for explanations of excess volatility. If it is just one sector that caused the volatility, it may be a short-term situation. If all, or most, sectors have shifted, this should definitely raise your suspicions. This article is right on the mark, noting that virtually all of the big components have dropped and the improvement has gone as far as it can go. So if you see largely downward numbers, you should suspect a recession (or the continuation of a down period). If you see largely an upswing in the numbers, you will likely have good times for the economy.

Want to get a bit sophisticated with your economic analysis? Do as the financial market participants do and look at the number of durable goods orders, excluding transportation. Transportation includes big components like military and civilian aircraft and space vehicles.[7] If orders are down for even one month, it can throw the entire monthly durable goods orders figure off and raise recessionary fears. Because these transportation orders are so large, they simply don't get placed on a regular basis. A big business may invest in an aircraft once every few years, not once a month. Even the Department of Defense works on a budget. It only purchases new tanks, ships, missiles, and the like on a scheduled basis. You get the picture—these items and their components are extremely costly and require careful planning before a purchase.

If You Want to Know More: Bureau of the Census M3 Report

The durable goods statistic is released in the monthly report by the Bureau of Census entitled Preliminary Report on Manufacturers' Shipments, Inventories, and Orders. In common usage this report is referred to as the "M3" report. Numbers for new orders and unfilled orders for durable goods and nondurable goods industries are in the M3 report.

The advance report is issued about three weeks after the end of the data month (along with a revision for the previous data month). For purposes of tracking, jot down the advance durable number. The preliminary report is available just over one month after the close of the reporting month. The data is subsequently revised one month later. Late surveys come in, and the preliminary report therefore may provide substantial revisions in durables. The stock or bond market however reacts to the early numbers in the advance release, and for our purposes the widely reported advance release (with updated revisions) will certainly alert you to the general trend.

These monthly numbers are subsequently revised based on annual benchmark information in the spring and released in the summer. Comprehensive benchmark revisions are made in most years.

Data for the M3 report is based on monthly surveys of manufacturers. The sample is based on most manufacturing companies with $500 million or more in annual shipments. Selected smaller companies are included to bolster the sample coverage for individual industries. The survey is mailed to the businesses to get an accurate sample base.

Bureau of the Census employees are diligent in their efforts. They call, send follow-up letters, and even make staff visits to collect the survey data. Based upon self-evaluation, each reporting company falls into one or more of eighty separately tabulated industry categories, based upon their primary business activities.

Chart 5-1

Manufacturers' New Orders, Durable Goods Industries

Business Cycle Activity

The Conference Board calculates a seasonally adjusted manufacturer's new orders for durable goods number (based on constant 1996 dollars), which is displayed in Chart 5-1.

The chart shows that durable goods tend to peak months before the economy falls into a recession; and the number falls steadily during the recessionary times. Here selection is down and so too will be sales. It bottoms out just before the economy starts its expansion and continues to rise during the expansionary phase.

Financial Participants' Reaction

Bond market participants know that a larger-than-expected increase in durable goods shows strength in manufacturing and GDP. Bond prices will fall because of anticipated strength in the U.S. economy. Bond players may grow concerned about rising inflation rates associated with increased growth and expect higher interest rates. Increased interest rates force down the prices of already issued bonds due to higher bond rates coming to market.

Again, the stock market reaction depends on interest rate fears. Strong orders are generally good and the market will often rise.

Nevertheless, all that said, durables are an interesting series. It is highly watched, but sometimes markets will not even react to the news. Financial markets know the series is volatile and often has big month-to-month shifts. If another indicator is sending a different message, participants may react to its data. With all the economic data out there, discerning exactly what news the market is reacting to is occasionally difficult. Market reaction often becomes an educated guessing game. One thing for sure, those heavily involved with the market will always be interested in the reports on durables. They need to know what is going on at the manufacturing level and if factories will start to roll. Sophisticated investors will also look at the durable goods orders, excluding some volatile components, such as transportation.[8]

Summary

There is a definite correlation between durable orders and domestic manufacturing production. When durable orders rise, it will ultimately cause manufacturers to increase production lines, and this means a boom for the economy. Conversely, when orders are down, manufacturing lines will become stagnant. This leads to tough times for the economy.

Durable Goods Orders is an important indicator of upcoming business trends. Time your shopping to coincide with an upswing, and you'll find increased selection and reduced prices. The opposite is also true. Generally, when durables are down, the selection is down and price moves up. That means it's better to hold on if you can.

Tracking Durable Goods Orders

Check out the durable goods number for some tips on timing your big-ticket purchases.

Frequency: The indicator is released on a monthly basis. Check the numbers for at least three months to get a feel for the trend.

When: The advance report on durable goods orders is released to the press early in the morning each month, roughly three weeks from the end of the data month. It is released along with a revision for the previous month, which you should jot down because oftentimes the revisions are notable.

Where: It is widely reported by national television news on the day of its release and the day following. CNNfn routinely covers the durable numbers. It generally runs the day following its release in many newspaper publications. For durables data, check out the *Washington Post,* the *New York Times,* and *USA Today,* all of which frequently cover the indicator. The number is usually available in the *Houston Chronicle,* the *Los Angeles Times,* the *Chicago Tribune,* the *Miami Herald,* the *Oregonian,* and Louisville's *Courier-Journal.* Other regional newspapers cover the number as news merits. Alternatively, you can get the number on the day following its release from *The Wall Street Journal* (in the Economy section) or *Investor's Business Daily* (in the Business & Economy section).

How: The press and television news generally will report the monthly dollar value of new orders for manufactured durable goods (such as $249.2 billion), a percentage change for the respective month (such as a 4.4 percent increase for July), or both. Look for commentary on the figures such as "largest increase on record" or "down month for big-ticket items."

Use the following chart to track durable goods orders:

Durable Goods Orders

January	
February	
March	
April	
May	
June	
July	
August	
September	
October	
November	
December	

Notes on Trend:

Chapter 6

Move or Redecorate?
Building Permits

"A man builds a fine house; and now he has a master, and a task for life is to furnish, watch, show it, and keep it in repair."

—Ralph Waldo Emerson

The purchase of a house is likely the single largest purchase you will make in your lifetime. It is truly part of the American dream—the house, two-car garage, and the white picket fence. People invest in the American dream when the economy is prosperous, and they feel comfortable spending large sums. It's a great time to sell your home and get top dollar. If you are buying during a boom, an existing home will probably offer you a better deal than building a new home. But when the economy gets tough, the housing market suffers and many people become unable to meet the mortgage payments on their homes. Here is where you are going to find your bargains.

The economy's highs and lows, reflected by GDP, are significantly more affected by the purchase of a new home than an existing home. Remember, only new purchases will go into GDP. Labor, bricks, lumber, and various other materials go into construction of a new home and all count toward the $9 trillion-plus annual GDP total. If you buy an existing home, the transaction does not count toward GDP. The house was already counted in GDP the first time it was sold, when it was built. Now, if you buy an existing home and make renovations, the materials and labor required for the upgrade will count toward GDP. While expenditures for improvements are significantly less than in building, in total, the residential housing industry accounts for a whopping 4.3 percent of GDP.

How can you get an early handle on the building activity that propels the economy? Take a look at the number of new building permits. A permit represents a plan to build and spend money on the construction of a new home. Permit issuance is the first step in the housing construction process and therefore has just a slightly longer lead time than housing starts (a start is counted on the date that the home construction is begun) for predicting recessions and expansions. Less than 5 percent of all privately owned housing units are built in areas of the country not requiring permits, so this number catches virtually all the homebuilding activity. Because of new housing construction, other businesses will prosper. The furniture store, appliance outlet, and carpet merchant will all experience brisk business filling new homes. It is such a strong leader, building permits is a component leading indicator for the Leading Economic Indicator (LEI).

While the sale of existing homes does not directly influence GDP, it is an enormous secondary market. As a rule, with a few exceptions, the sales of new homes and existing homes move up or down together. When we enter a recession, the entire housing market will universally taper off. And when we enter an expansion, the housing market will take off.

So before you sell your house and move to a larger home, make a decision between a new home or an existing home, choose home ownership over apartment living, put on an addition to your home, or even redecorate your home, take a look at the monthly building permit indicator. Building permit numbers provide insight into housing and the overall economy.

Where to Find Building Permits

The monthly building permits data is always released jointly with housing starts. For any given month, its data is made publicly available on the morning of the twelfth working day of the following month. The number is often published with a revision for the previous month, so update your figures if you catch the revision. You can also get the permits number on the national television business news on the day of its release and the day after. CNNfn routinely reports on monthly building permits. Newspapers generally report on the number on the day after its release. You will find it in big circulation newspapers such as the *New York Times*, the *Washington Post*, or in *USA Today*, where it is sometimes covered as part of a story on housing activity. Most regional and local newspapers cover this number only when they deem the news merits attention.

If you miss the news, you can catch the number in *The Wall Street Journal* (in the Economy section) and in *Investor's Business Daily* (in the Business & Economy section) on the day following its release.[1] Alternatively, you can call (212) 339-0330 for a recorded message listing building permits.

For planning your housing decisions, it is recommended that you check the numbers for at least three months in order to get a feel for the trend.

What the Number Says

Besides contributing to feelings of prosperity or doom, interest rates have an effect on your decision to buy a home. Past history suggests that interest rates rise during expansions and fall during recessions. Interest rates tend to be at their lowest at the bottom of a recession and highest when the economy peaks.[2] Historical data suggests that building permits signal an economic expansion an average of six months ahead of time. Ultimately, the timing for a boom period in the economy becomes just right. As interest rates are in a low range in the recession and people begin to experience some increase in their incomes, they make the decision to build a new house. Traffic at the local permit office swells. Permits will begin an upward rise (from its low point), and in a few months, the economy will be out of a recession and entering an expansionary phase. Due to the overwhelming feelings of prosperity, coupled with the wide availability of adjustable-rate mortgages (home loans in which the rate will change based upon the economy and fluctuating market interest rates), the number of building permits will continue to surge. People will still build new houses, even when mortgage rates hit double-digits, because their incomes are thriving and they know the adjustable rate will fall if the economy gets tough again. Certainly now is the time to sell your house—and sell high! But during expansions, there tends to be a strong consumer preference for new homes rather than existing homes. So if you're buying a house, pick out a great existing home for the best deal.

But all good things must come to an end. Building permits give an average recession warning of just over twenty-two months. Building permits will peak and begin a downward plunge in the later part of the expansionary phase. The still-high interest rates joined with an initial pinch in the pocketbook is a bad combination. The number of qualified borrowers will be reduced by the high interest rates (raising the cost of borrowing) and the fall in income. The drop in new home construction helps push the economy into a recession. Interest rates will fall, but the number of new building permits will continue to drop off too. Even though rates are down, many people are unable to make such a large purchase in dreary economic times because they have not planned ahead.

But herein lies the trick to using permits. Permits can alert you to the general trend in housing. When permits are tapering off, there is not as much building activity. The economy is about to turn down and soon there is going to be a glut of homes on the market. You can find some steals in the housing market, but it is a bad time to list your home. At the same time, it is a great time to add that addition because carpenters and construction workers will give you a great deal. They need the work, and their phones quit ringing a while back. Even if you wait until we are in the midst of a recession, you will benefit from low, low interest rates. That's great news not only for those buying a house but for individuals renovating and taking out a home equity loan. Now, this does take a bit of planning, but that is the beauty of the building permits indicator. The long time span gives you adequate time to plan your housing decisions.

Using Building Permits

Virtually everyone has some type of housing concern. Let's take a glimpse at some of the major decisions that plague our minds when it comes to the all-important home. Is it a good time to sell and move to a larger house? This is a complex question because along with buying a larger house you must sell your current home. And the old adage "buy low, sell high" certainly applies to the costly housing market. Consider hiring a qualified real estate appraiser to help you determine what you can expect to receive for your current home—based on the economy, interest rates, and local market conditions. When you have a good idea what you can sell your house for, you can more easily gauge your spending limit for the larger home. But keep in mind that, as a general rule, an economic down time is a bad time to sell your home because you won't get top dollar. It is, however, a good time to buy. So timing is all-important. Watch the trend of building permits and housing construction and sales in your town. If you see permits have hit a high point and are in a notable downward progression, you can expect that very shortly the economy will move out of an expansion. Capitalize on the strong economy and sell in the high range. Sell for such a great price that you can easily afford a larger and nicer home. As permits taper off, you will see some early signs of housing sluggishness in the economy. Buy the new big house from the overextended builder. And certainly go for the adjustable-rate mortgage because rates are going down, down, down.

Should you buy a new home or an existing home? If you are in a situation where you need to buy a home quickly—a tax consequence or a company move—then you will be buying regardless of the economic situation. You need to make the current economy work for you. In the midst of a recession or at the height an expansion, you have to get the best deal possible. Well you can. And again, building permits can provide some direction. When permits are low and the economy has turned down, you will have the pick of the market. Maybe you like fixer-uppers, established neighborhood dwellings, or historic homes. Go for your favorite. When the country enters a recession, many homeowners won't be able to keep paying the mortgage and upkeep on their nice homes. Business has tapered off, and sales commissions plummet. People have their hours greatly reduced. And sadly, many people lose their jobs. Deals are abundant in the existing home market. Interested in buying a new home when building is down? During a recession, the number of months it takes from the start of a single-family home to its ultimate sale extends from 3.6 months in non-recession years to 4.6 months for recession years. The longer a home sits, the more willing the builder is to negotiate on price. You can bet the builder is anxious to deal because he has a great deal of money invested in the house and he wants out. That extra month is costing him big time in interest payments. So find a great spec house that has been sitting on the market for a while. With a bit of wheeling and dealing, it can be yours at a great price.

But if permits are high, and the country is in the throes of an expansion, you can still find a bargain home. You are just going to have to be a bit craftier to find a good deal. Consult with local builders, bankers, and real estate agents about the housing trend in your city. Visit subdivisions with new homes and established neighborhoods. Is the city overbuilt by new homebuilders? Or maybe there is a wonderful established neighborhood with well-preserved homes at low prices. There is a recognizable preference for new homes, compared to existing homes, during an expansion. People have a heightened sense of prosperity and often want brand-new homes. If the demand for new homes starts to rise (one way you notice this is if new homes start to sell more quickly), the prices of new homes will start to creep up. Play it safe, and go with a previously owned home.

Is it a good idea to add on? First and foremost, you must consider if you can easily add the features you need to your existing home. Adding a sunroom, patio, or extra bedroom is probably feasible. But if you have your heart set on a basement or a second floor, construction is going to be much more costly and significantly trickier. Will the addition increase the selling price of your home? If you aren't going to be able to get your money out of the renovation when you sell, then the addition is not a practical idea. But if it is something you want and the addition will increase the value of your home, then go for it. For a low quote, wait for just the right time. If it is a downtime for permits, construction workers and carpenters really feel the pain because they are probably not working. New homes are a big part of their business. So you can likely contract a terrific deal for that addition. Not only will the workers be at your house every day and complete the job on schedule (you don't have to vie for their attention the way you do when home building is booming), but you can now get a low interest rate on the home equity loan for the addition.

Apartment or house, which way should you go? The advantages of owning a home are many—a refuge, a safe haven, and, most likely, your largest asset. But don't automatically assume that home ownership is the smartest option. Analyze what the building permits number is telling you so you can make an educated decision. While researching on the Internet, you discover that the recent steady upward progression of permits suggests that the economy is about to move up, too. You recall that permits start to turn up on average six months before the economy. Okay, you are armed with some essential information. Did you know that in a prosperous, booming economy it might make more sense to rent an apartment? You can take the money you save by renting and invest it (wisely, of course). Ride the expansion. If you can hold out until permits start to fall and a recession is upon the country (the average recession warning is over twenty-two months), you will be in a better position to buy a home that might have been prohibitively priced just a few months before.

Should you redecorate your home instead of moving? If you are a do-it-yourself decorator, be smart and take on the challenge when permits are high. The economy is strong and so too is your pocketbook. You are much more likely to spend freely and do it right. If, however, you are going to hire any type of help for the home improvements, take another glance at building permits. Wait until permits hit a low point and then phone the decorator. Most of a decorator's work comes from new homes being built. In a downtime for new construction, a decorator will be available and will offer better fees or lower commissions. Have you ever tried to get a painter to work on your home during a boom period? Forget it. During a strong economy, painters are subcontracted by home builders. Those who make a living heavily connected to new home construction are certainly affected by the level of building permits. So if you are going to hire, wait until permits are down.

American consumers spent nearly $300 billion on furniture and household equipment in 1999. That is about $1,063 of new furniture and household equipment for every man, woman, and child in the United States.

In 1999, more than five million existing homes were sold, along with just under one million new single-family houses. Housing is a big, expensive business! A peek at building permits can provide a hint of the trend for the housing industry. So before you invest your life savings in a home or pour significant cash into renovating or redecorating, view building permits. Like many things in life, with the housing industry, timing is everything.

Compilation and Release of the Number

Building permits is technically referred to as the total U.S. authorization of new private housing units by local building permits. Exactly what is a housing unit? Is it a single home, apartment, or duplex? The answer is that it is all three and more. The definition of a housing unit reads:

A housing unit is a house, an apartment, a group of rooms or a single room intended for occupancy as separate living quarters. Separate living quarters are those in which the occupants live separately from any other individuals in the building and which have a direct access from the outside of the building or through a common hall.[3]

Okay, so what is excluded from the data? First of all, these building permits are for new home construction only; additions and renovations don't count. Mobile homes are not included in the building permit data. Publicly owned housing is not included either. Further, the data relates to new housing units designed for living on a housekeeping basis. So motels, hotels, and college dorms are all examples of living units not meeting the definition of a housing unit.

Now that you have a better understanding of what is meant by "housing," let's take a look at the data. Housing is definitely a seasonal business. There is a great deal more building in summer, spring, and fall than in winter. Because seasonal factors, particularly poor weather conditions, affect housing data, building permit numbers are seasonally adjusted.[4] And although the reporting agency calculates both non–seasonally adjusted and seasonally adjusted numbers, the seasonally adapted figures are most efficient for spotting trends and are always reported by the press.

When the January 2000 building permits and housing starts data were released to the press on February 16, 2000, immediately the Dow Jones News Service reported on the solid numbers. In a common reporting practice, permits and starts (there is a definite correlation between the two over time) are both mentioned in the same story. Following is a section of the report that discusses housing activity, where permits and starts are both nearing the high 1.8 million annual range:

> U.S. housing starts began 2000 with surprising resiliency, climbing to their highest level in a year on strength in the multifamily housing sector.
>
> The Commerce Department said Wednesday housing starts grew 1.5% to a seasonally adjusted 1.775 million annual rate in January, providing more evidence that rising interest rates, and even inclement weather in January, were unable to derail a robust housing market.
>
> Building permits, seen as a precursor of future housing activity, were up 8.7% in January to a 1.763 million annual rate, also the highest monthly level since January 1999.[5]

When we analyze the monthly permit data, we are looking for trends up or down. Be cautious in analyzing trends because month-to-month changes in statistics often show movements that may be irregular. Higher and lower than normally expected seasonal shifts do occur. For example, the winter may be much worse than ever anticipated and accounted for in seasonally adjusted numbers. Even the reporting agency cautions that it may take five months to establish an underlying trend for total starts and three months for building permit authorizations. So don't jump to any automatic conclusions about the economic trend until you have observed permits over a number of months.

For example, looking at a six-month span from August 1999 through January 2000, annually adjusted permits, except for one initial plunge down, were largely on an upward progression: 1.619 million, 1.506 million, 1.594 million, 1.612 million, 1.622 million, and 1.763 million, respectively. This is in keeping with the lengthy economic expansion that the country had been experiencing. Be cautious before predicting downturns or upturns. For example, even in the midst of an expansion, you will have down months, often in an erratic pattern. Even in this brief string of numbers you see the second month, September permits, taking a dip and the numbers steadily rising from the dip. It is very common to have down months or even a brief down period. Don't suspect an upcoming recession until you see many months of falling permits.

You recall that permits start falling, on average, just over twenty-two months before a recession hits. Looking back at the beginning of the January 1980 to July 1980 recession, you can see that building permits (seasonally adjusted annual rate) started to turn down roughly nineteen months ahead of the economy's peak. Note that permits hit a high point in June 1978, roughly nineteen months prior to the economy's downturn, and began a sometimes bumpy downward descent.

Permits

May 1978	1,766,000
June 1978	1,983,000
July 1978	1,786,000
August 1978	1,691,000

Although it is not always simple to discern a definitive trend, watching the monthly permit numbers will provide you with a strong hint about upcoming housing and economic activity. That is all numbers can provide—a suspicion or clue about upcoming activity. So with permits, faithfully watch the monthly numbers; but just as loyally monitor new subdivisions in your town, building activity in your area, and sales of new and existing homes there. Get the local scoop from your friendly real estate agent and mortgage loan officer. Knowledge of the numbers coupled with data on the local front will give you the information you need to make the costly home-related decisions.

If You Want to Know More:
The Residential Construction Branch of the Census Bureau

A branch of the U.S. Census Bureau, Residential Construction, provides the monthly building permit data. The data comes from a survey mailed to local building permit officials. Monthly statistics are based on data from a sample of approximately eighty-five hundred to nine thousand permit offices. Annual statistics are compiled from all nineteen thousand permit offices. This information is available from the Census Bureau website (www.census.gov/const/c40). Preliminary starts/permits data is released on the twelfth working day of the month, at 8:30 A.M. Eastern Time, in a press release entitled "C20 Housing Starts/Building Permits."

A revised number to the monthly number of building permits is made on the eighteenth working day of the month, in the "C40 Building Permits" press release. This report does not receive widespread press coverage. You can, however, get the data from the Census Bureau website or easily catch it the next month with the new preliminary numbers.

So that you can contrast the preliminary and revised numbers for January 2000 data, both are listed on the following chart. As you can see from this sample, the preliminary and revised numbers do vary somewhat, but not significantly. If you catch the revision, go ahead and update the numbers for technical accuracy.

Chart 6-1

Privately Owned Housing Units Authorized by Building Permits
January 2000 (Thousands of Units)
Season Adjusted Annual Rate

		In structures with			Geographic area			
Period	Total	1 unit	2-4 units	5 units or more	Northeast	Midwest	South	West
Preliminary	1,763	1,303	62	398	198	381	754	430
Revised	1,772	1,318	65	389	191	379	759	443

Source: U.S. Department of Commerce Bureau of the Census

There are a number of limitations to the building permit data. Occasionally, a small amount of work in building permit areas slips by the recording process. Boundaries in local permit areas can change due to new incorporations and annexations. Therefore, such data would not be strictly comparable. Some permit offices may close the books a few days before the calendar month actually ends. All limitations are minor and do not materially alter the capacity of the series to foretell economic turns.

As previously mentioned, the monthly estimates of building permits is based on a sample of eighty-five hundred to nine thousand permit offices. Sometime after the first of the year, a questionnaire goes to the remaining ten thousand or so offices. The Census Bureau compiles and releases the annual final figure on the first working day of May. Revisions to seasonal factors are published each May and generally go back for two years.

You can see from Chart 6-1 that the Residential Construction branch further divides housing data into single and multifamily units. Total housing data is reclassified on a regional basis as well—Northeast, Midwest, South, and West. Each housing unit is counted individually, so a five hundred–unit apartment complex counts as five hundred units. Multifamily classification is grouped into two units, three and four units (two to four units were combined in the January release), and five units or more. Most of the units are single units, around 74 percent. Over time, the single unit component is less volatile. For our purposes, the total number of building permits is an excellent indicator of recession or expansion. If, however, you are interested in a more detailed economic analysis, along with the total permits number, monitor permits for single-family units. The data is easily accessible from the Census Bureau website. The point of volatility in multifamily units is easy to see. A new five hundred–unit apartment complex can quickly inflate the numbers and skew the residential construction numbers. The building of the large apartment complex is most likely the whim of one builder or one corporation, where construction of five hundred new single-family homes is at the whim of five hundred families, and those five hundred families have spending power.

Building Permits Is a Choice Leading Indicator

The two housing series that are most widely watched are building permits and housing starts. What is the difference? The building permit is required prior to construction. Housing starts represent actual housing construction. The Census Bureau reports that construction begins for all but a very small percentage of permits.

In actuality, the two are highly correlated. Permits and starts act as leading indicators at both peaks and troughs. Most construction, or starts, begins the same month the building permit is issued. Further, most of the remainder begin construction within the three following months. You can imagine a multitude of tiny events that delay construction: poor weather conditions, shifting mortgage rates, and labor shortages, to name just a few. So although both permits and starts are good indicators to watch for insight into business cycle movements, this book has chosen to track building permits. It is favored mainly because it is the first step in the housing construction process and therefore has a slightly longer lead-time at peaks and troughs. Also, it is advisable to watch five months of starts for a trend, but permits require only three months of tracking.

Business Cycle Activity

Building Permits hits its peak an average of 22.1 months prior to the economy's peak, before the economy enters into a recession. On the other hand, Building Permits bottoms out six months, on average, before the economy hits bottom and subsequently starts expanding.[6] You can see from Chart 6-2 that the series falls dramatically during recessions and takes off during expansionary periods.

Chart 6-2

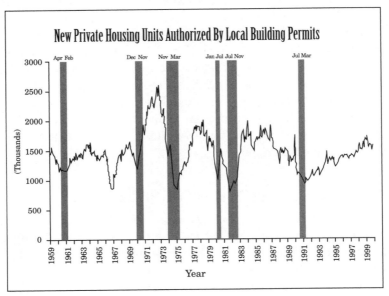

New Private Housing Units Authorized By Local Building Permits

Building permits are uniquely tied to the economy. When permits are falling, housing tapers off and the economy goes into a recession. But when permits take off again, the economy starts moving up.

Financial Participants' Reaction

Preliminary data for building permits is released with housing starts. The financial markets usually react to the general trend of the preliminary report. Namely, a weak housing report—falling permits and starts—causes the bond market to react positively. A weak report suggests dampening economic growth and no inflationary pressure. Bond prices will rise with such news. On the other hand, a strong housing report—rising permits and starts—is bad news for the bond market because it hints at increased inflation. This causes bond prices to fall.

Stock market participants watch for the Census Bureau release and generally react in the opposite manner. A positive report of rising permits and starts says the economy is moving in a strong direction. As long as there are no overriding interest rate and inflationary fears, the stock market will likely move upward on the information. What is the assumption? Strong housing will translate into strong residential and spin-off spending. A poor housing report tells investors that people aren't spending on new construction of houses and apartment buildings and will likely cause the market to fall.

Summary

A building permit, the first step in the home building process, is required prior to home construction. Permits foretell economic upturns and downturns. Permits authorization for housing construction is big business. There are currently roughly 1.8 million permits issued each year.

When permits are low, there is not much building activity. The economy is about to turn down, and soon there is going to be a glut of homes on the market. You can find some bargains in the housing market, but it is a bad time to list your home. It is, however, a great time to add that addition because carpenters and construction workers will give you good deals. They need the work and also are more available to get it done for you on schedule. If you wait until the economy is in recession, you get low, low interest rates. That is great news not only for those buying a house but for individuals taking out a home equity loan to renovate or redecorate.

When permits are high, housing is booming and so is the economy. People will still build new houses, even when mortgage rates hit double-digits, because their incomes are thriving. In addition, they count on adjustable rates falling if the economy gets tough. This is not going to be the best time to build a new home or buy an existing house. But if you are buying in an expanding economy you will likely notice a buyers' preference for new homes compared to existing homes. An existing home will offer a better deal. If you sell your house during an expansion, it will bring in the big bucks. Housing permits provide useful information to you when you're buying, selling, or renovating a home.

Tracking Building Permits

Check out the Building Permits indicator for tips on home buying and selling.

Frequency: The indicator is released on a monthly basis. Check the numbers for at least three months to get a feel for the trend.

When: Building permits data is always released jointly with housing starts. The information is made publicly available on the morning of the twelfth working day of the month following the month being covered. The number oftentimes is published with a revision for the previous month; if you catch the revision, it is a good idea to update the figures.

Where: Catch it on the national television business news on the day of its release and the day after. CNNfn routinely reports on monthly building permits. Newspapers generally report on the number the day after its release. You will find it in big circulation newspapers such as the *New York Times,* the *Washington Post,* or *USA Today* where it is sometimes covered as part of a story on housing activity. Most regional newspapers cover this number as news merits. Alternatively, you can find it in *The Wall Street Journal* (in the Economy section) or *Investor's Business Daily* (in the Business & Economy section) on the day following its release. Or call (212) 339-0330 for a recorded message that lists building permits.

How: The press and television news generally will report the number of housing units authorized by building permits expressed at a seasonally adjusted annual rate (such as 1,658,000), a percentage change for the respective month (such as a 3 percent decrease for December), or both. Look for commentary on the figures, such as "virtually unchanged since last month" or "strong showing for the housing sector."

Use the following chart to track building permits:

Building Permits

January	
February	
March	
April	
May	
June	
July	
August	
September	
October	
November	
December	

Notes on Trend:

Chapter 7

Investing in 90 Percent of the Market: S&P 500

"Let Wall Street have a nightmare and the whole country has to help get them back in bed again."

—Will Rogers

There are a multitude of stock market averages that measure the movement of the market.[1] The Dow Jones Industrial Average (DJIA) is one popular indicator of daily stock market change, but it contains only thirty representative stocks. For the best quick read on the vast market, check out the Standard & Poor's 500. The S&P 500, as it is commonly known, has a total of five hundred stocks in its average, so it provides a wide view of the stock market. And it measures top firms in all the leading industries—retail, auto, chemical, pharmaceuticals, publishing, banking, manufacturing, and computers, to name just a few. The index, dominated by strong blue-chip firms, has a total market value of $11.5 trillion. That value approximates just over 90 percent of the value of the stocks listed on the entire New York Stock Exchange. Further, the firms in the S&P 500 represent close to 75 percent of the investment-grade equities held by typical institutional money managers.

What does movement in the stock market mean? The S&P 500 hits its high point an average of six months prior to a recession. The index and its representative stocks fall during the recession as investors become skeptical about the economy's performance and sell their stocks. Selling puts downward pressure on stock prices. This is the best time to be buying stocks, because if the S&P 500 is down, it is likely the stocks you are interested in are down as well. Except for normal fluctuations, stock prices will stay depressed during the recession. Then, an average of four months before the economy picks up, the S&P 500 starts moving upward. The upward takeoff will extend during the expansion. During an expansion, investors are optimistic about the economy and buy stocks. This buying momentum puts upward pressure on the price of stocks. Now is the time to sell, when the prices of stocks are hot. When the S&P 500 is up and your stocks are in demand is the time to cash in.

And there is more. The S&P 500's rates of return over the last five years have posted an average annual return of 25.14 percent, and the last ten years have averaged an annual return of 18.05 percent. So look to movements in the S&P index if you are investing in stocks or are interested in doing so. Help with your stock market investments is right here in one number that is easy to interpret and is widely accessible. As a general rule, the bigger the investment amount, the longer the amount of time you should track the S&P 500. Before making any major buying and selling decisions, try to track data for six months to one year.

Where to Find the S&P 500

The daily S&P 500 is easily made available by local and national television programs. CNNfn gives wide coverage to this indicator. Or, you can look it up in the business sections of most local, regional, or national newspapers. You can catch it daily in big newspapers such as the *New York Times,* the *Washington Post,* or *USA Today* as well as from regional publications like the *Miami Herald,* the *Los Angeles Times,* the *Chicago Tribune,* the *San Jose Mercury News,* Louisville's *Courier-Journal,* the *Oregonian,* the *Tampa Tribune,* or the *Houston Chronicle.*

If you miss the news coverage, both *The Wall Street Journal* and *Investor's Business Daily* list the S&P 500 on the front page, details appear inside. You can also call (800) 592-6051 for information on the index.

For planning your stock-related moves, you should check the number frequently during the month for at least one month in order to get a feel for the trend.

What the Number Says

The S&P 500 is a market-weighted index. It is easy to compute: stock price times the number of shares outstanding. The level of the S&P 500 index is simply the total market value of all the five hundred stocks included in the index. The index includes companies selected by the

Standard & Poor's Index Committee to reflect the stock market. Many of the company names on the index will be familiar to you: Boeing Company, General Motors, Anheuser-Busch, Coca-Cola Co., Kmart, IBM, Dow Chemical, and Wal-Mart, to name but a few.

The S&P 500 index currently hovers near 1,500. The value of the S&P 500 index today is roughly a whopping 150 times the value it was in the years 1941 to 1943. Now how's that for one fine return?

When stock market traders are positive about the economy, they will buy. This pushes the stock market up, and the value of the index will rise. Now even on an up day for the S&P 500, some stocks may finish at the same price as the day before and some may fall. But this heightened number tells you that the overriding trend of the market was up. On the flip side, stock players anticipating tough economic times will sell, and this drives the market down so the S&P 500 will fall. And too, you will have some stocks that will stay level and some may rise, but the trend is down. This one simple measure gives you an indication of movement for the entire market. It is such a good leader of the economy, The Conference Board has chosen to include the S&P 500 as one of its ten leading indicators.

So if you want to invest in stocks, there is no better stock indicator to monitor for upturns or downturns in the economy than the S&P 500. And with an annual historical return of over 25 percent, the S&P 500 is hard to beat. So let's check out how the S&P 500 can work for you.

Using the S&P 500

There are many fine books that will help you decide on a strategy to pick the stocks you want to own in your portfolio. In addition, there are now thousands of mutual funds whose managers will make those decisions on your behalf. However, whether you are working with a broker, investing in individual stocks online, or investing in mutual funds, you will want to watch the S&P 500 to stay informed about market trends. This will help you decide whether to take your broker's advice about buying and selling, when the time to act is if you're an online investor, and whether or not you should consider switching mutual funds.

Before we discuss this stock market index, there are just a few basic concepts you need to know. First of all, when we talk about stock we are referring to common shares in a company. When you buy common stock shares of a company you actually own some of the business. You will be part owner of BestBuy Co., Eastman Kodak, or Apple Computer, for example. If the corporation is prosperous and pays a dividend, you will receive a dividend check every three months.[2] The notable thing about common stock is the dividend has the potential to move upward as strong firms typically reward stockholders by periodically increasing dividends. These stocks are known as "income" stocks because the dividend generates income for you. "Growth" stocks pay small dividends, or sometimes no dividends at all, but are expected to grow significantly in value. Again, there are many books on stock investing that will give you a great introduction to the stock market. Consult your local bookstore or library for specific titles. The key thing to know is that as long as you own a company's stock, you will always own part of that firm, unless the company goes bankrupt and ceases to exist. As the economy and your company prosper, the price of the stock will further increase in value.

The purpose of monitoring the S&P 500 is to maximize the earning power of your stock investments. If you are a long-term investor not interested in actively buying and selling, buy a representative sample of the S&P 500 stocks and hold them for the long term. Investment analysts commonly recommend diversifying by buying a minimum of ten different stocks, from different industry segments.[3] However, if you are interested in pursuing a stock strategy to truly maximize your wealth, the S&P 500 offers excellent signals. Overall, buy when the market is down and sell when the market is up. The S&P 500 starts to plummet roughly six months, on average, prior to a recession and falls off during the recession. This is your buy signal, plain and simple. You want to be buying at a downtime for the market. Stock investors are skeptical about the economy's performance and sell their stocks. This selling pressure puts downward pressure on the price of stocks. If the S&P 500 is down, it is likely the stocks you are interested in are down as well. When you suspect that the S&P 500 is on a steady movement up, quit buying.

Approximately four months, on average, prior to the economy's upturn, the S&P 500 will pick up. Here you have an extra hint that the upturn has hit. News reports often comment on increased share trading. If you hear that three, four, or even five times the normal volume of shares is being traded, you may have a signal that the market has bottomed out. Verify by checking out a daily financial publication for the total share volume for the New York Stock Exchange. During an expansion, investors feel strongly about the economy and buy stocks. This forceful buying puts pressure on the price of stocks and they rise, often feverishly. Now is your time to trade. Sell stocks during a hot expansion when everybody wants them.

If you need a reliable income, you can still invest in the stock market. The stock market offers great opportunities for people who want to earn the great returns but need a reliable income. The majority of stocks do pay dividends, but dividends may taper off when times are tough. If you rely on stock income to live, you must buy companies that have a steady source of income, even during downtimes. Go with businesses that are referred to as defensive stocks. You need firms that have stable earnings and are able to maintain dividends even during recessions. Big business categories that are commonly defensive include high-grade banking firms, health care, and utilities (electric companies and natural gas providers). Just think about it. Banks notoriously do well because they make their money on interest spreads, the difference between the money they charge you for a loan and what they pay you for your deposit. If times get tough and loan rates fall, they will lower what they pay you on your deposit. Profitable banks are very skilled at managing the spread. If you need medicine, medical care, or health care supplies, you are buying regardless of the state of the economy. And people are always going to pay their utility bills (gas and electricity) before spending the money elsewhere. The S&P 500 includes a long list of these firms that are very strong. And because these industries are mainstays, the price appreciation comes as well. Further, while banks, health-care firms, and utility companies' stock prices may rise and fall with the economic cycle, they tend not to take too much of a beating during a recession—remember, they are defensive. So you won't get your best recession steals here. Check out one of the many investors' business publications, or take a look at the Standard & Poor's index services website for defensive buys. Do your own research on these stocks and look at their past dividend track records as an indication of future payout ratios.

If you need cash and are wondering when the best time would be to get out of the stock market, generally you want to watch the S&P closely for the general trend up or down. You definitely want to sell high. This generally occurs when the S&P is high and the country is in an expansion. If you hear on the news that the country is likely coming out of a recession and the S&P has started to pick up, postpone selling, if you can. Wait until the country is fully immersed in the expansion. The price of stocks typically keeps rising throughout the prosperous period.

But if you feel your stock has captured most of its upward potential, you don't want to hold on too long. An expansion will eventually turn into a recession and then you will have missed your selling opportunity. Remember, as a general rule, just a few months before the end of the expansion, the S&P 500 will start its downward journey. So if you are watching the economic indicators and you judge that the S&P 500 and the economy are going to turn shortly, get out while the getting is good.

Here's how to maximize your stock-buying dollar. If you buy during a recession when the S&P 500 has hit bottom, you will get the best bargain prices. Still, maximize your dollar and go for the cyclical stocks. Most of these stocks are in heavy industries such as: automobiles, metals (aluminum, iron, and steel), machinery, manufacturing, and paper. They are generally manufacturing related and thus have huge fixed expenses.[4] When the economy is strong, so too are these firms, because they have no difficulty covering the vast expenses of maintaining manufacturing facilities. But when the economy dips, the manufacturing lines remain idle but the costs are still there. So the price of these companies' stocks can really tumble. While you can get a good buy on most any stock during a recession, these heavy industry cyclical stocks can offer even better opportunities. Hold them during the recession, watch the prices rebound, and sell them before another recession hits. Just ask yourself what companies are hurting most when the economy is down. And if these companies have the potential to recover when the economy rebounds, you have yourself a deal.

The S&P 500 is reported widely every day, often accompanied by commentary on the direction of the market, so the information is readily available to you whenever you want to look into it.

Compilation and Release of the Number

The S&P 500, which dates back to 1926, is volatile on a daily basis. Daily fluctuations in demand and supply of stocks cause the S&P 500 to constantly shift throughout the day and from day to day. Therefore, look at the number frequently to spot a long-term overriding dip or rise.

There are never any revisions to the S&P 500 numbers. And the index always consists of five hundred firms, but changes in the specific firms frequently occur. Deletions and subsequent additions are commonly reported in financial publications. Firms are deleted from the S&P 500 for the following four reasons: merger with or acquisition by another firm, bankruptcy, restructuring, or the firm is no longer considered to be representative of its industry group.

Following is an example of a press release showing the adjustment of the representative stocks, along with an explanation for doing so:

SABRE HOLDINGS CORPORATION ADDED TO S&P 500 INDEX
New York, NY, March 8, 2000 Standard & Poor's will replace Service Corp. International (NYSE:SRV) in the S&P 500 Index with Sabre Holdings Corporation (NYSE:TSG) after the close of trading on Wednesday, March 15, 2000. Service Corp. International is being

removed for lack of representation. S&P 500 component AMR Corp. (NYSE) is spinning off its 83 percent interest in Sabre Holdings to AMR shareholders.

Sabre Holdings Corporation is a holding company which engages in the electronic distribution of travel through its proprietary computer reservation system, Sabre (R). The company, headquartered in Fort Worth, Texas, will be added to the S&P 500 Services (Computer Systems) industry group.[5]

Following is a summary of the announced changes:

S&P 500 INDEX: March 15, 2000

	Company	Economic Sector	Industry Group
Added	Sabre Holdings Corp.	Technology	Services (Computer Systems)
Dropped	Service Corp. International	Consumer Cyclicals	Services (Commercial & Consumer)

Source: Standard & Poor's press release (March 8, 2000)

On the Standard & Poor's website you can find detailed listings of all 500 companies. Firms are classified into four major groupings. The overwhelming majority—roughly three-fourths—of the companies fall into the industrials category. Here are some sample firms in each category:

- **Industrials:** Boeing Company, Ford Motor, and Colgate-Palmolive.

- **Utilities:** Edison International, Southern Co., and El Paso Energy.

- **Financials:** Bank of New York, American Express, and Countrywide Credit Industries.

- **Transportation:** Norfolk Southern Corp., Ryder Systems, and Southwest Airlines.

Most of the representative stocks (448) come from the NYSE, and the remaining fifty-two are from NASDAQ. The nation's largest organized exchange, the NYSE, is home to 3,025 firms with more than $12.3 trillion in market value. Also known as the "Big Board," the NYSE is located on Wall Street. Because of the exchange's stringent listing requirements, companies listed tend to be the largest and best-known firms. The organization was founded in 1792, and trading actually took place under an old buttonwood tree facing 68 Wall Street. In 1817, the name "The New York Stock Exchange" (NYSE) was adopted. The exchange also holds the unique distinction of being the largest stock marketplace in the world.

Unlike the NYSE trading, there is no physical location for the trading of the over-the-counter NASDAQ stocks. Over-the-counter trading, otherwise known as the OTC market, largely conducts business through an electronic marketplace run by the National Association of Securities Dealers. Brokers view the OTC market on computer screens and trade with other brokers via the phone. The National Association of Securities Dealers Automatic Quotation (NASDAQ) system lists 4,814 companies with a total market value of $6.1 trillion, ranging from small growth companies to large firms. There are also thousands more smaller traded stocks in the OTC market. These stocks are not listed with NASDAQ and trade so infrequently that brokers receive hard copy pink sheets that list the trading information on the stocks. (Yes, the sheets really are pink!) Alternatively, brokers can subscribe to an electronic service that lists the information about the less frequently traded stocks.

> The first stock exchange in America? Philadelphia in 1790. Much of the early revenue of the exchange came from fines. Members who broke the exchange's code of civility and common decency were charged a fine of $1.00 for profane language. Whistling on the exchange floor would set members back $.10. And those who dared to wind the clock without permission of the president were assessed a whopping fine of $5.00.

Just a few months before an expansion, the S&P 500 index will start to turn up. This is a signal that soon the economy will be expanding, and when the S&P 500 reaches heightened levels it will be time to sell. Take a look at Chart 7-1 to view the heightened 1999–2000 rates of the S&P 500 (a monthly average). The index has been on a fast-and-furious upsurge for the last decade. Its growth, even over a matter of months, is obvious.

Chart 7-1

INDEX OF STOCK PRICES
(not seasonally adjusted)
500 Common Stocks

January 1999	1,248.77
February 1999	1,246.58
March 1999	1,281.66
April 1999	1,344.76
May 1999	1,332.07
June 1999	1,332.07
July 1999	1,380.99
August 1999	1,327.49
September 1999	1,318.17
October 1999	1,300.01
November 1999	1,391.00
December 1999	1,428.68
January 2000	1,425.59
February 2000	1,388.87
March 2000	1,422.21
April 2000	1,461.36
May 2000	1,418.48

Source: U.S. Department of Commerce Bureau of Economic Analysis and Standard and Poor's. Inc.

Right before a recession, the S&P will start falling. Drops are your important buy signals. A notable and sustained dip should raise your suspicions of a depressed period.

If You Want to Know More: S&P 500 Returns

Over five years, roughly from 1995 to 1999, the S&P 500 posted a spectacular average annual return of 25.14 percent. The ten years from approximately 1989 to 1999 averaged an outstanding annual return of 18.05 percent.

S&P Stock Indexes

Standard & Poor's currently publishes ten U.S. stock indexes along with a multitude of international stock indexes. Included are four component measures of the S&P 500: S&P 500 Industrials, S&P 500 Transportation, S&P 500 Utilities, and S&P 500 Financials. You can find information on the S&P indexes in financial publications. Following is a brief description of each index:

- **S&P 500:** Measures a representative sample of top firms in leading industries.

- **S&P 500 Industrials:** A component indicator measuring the industrials segment of the S&P 500.

- **S&P 500 Transportation:** A component indicator measuring the transportation segment of the S&P 500.

- **S&P 500 Utilities:** A component indicator measuring the utilities segment of the S&P 500.

- **S&P 500 Financial:** A component indicator measuring the financial segment of the S&P 500.

- **S&P 100:** Measures large company "blue chip" stock performance.

- **S&P 400 Mid Cap:** Measures the performance of mid-size firms.

- **S&P 600 Small Cap:** Measures the performance of small-size firms.

- **S&P SuperComposite 1500 Index:** A combination of the S&P 500, Mid Cap 400, and Small Cap 600.

- **S&P REIT Composite:** Measures the performance of Real Estate Investment Trusts, chosen for diversification and liquidity.

Business Cycle Activity

As you can see from Chart 7-2, the S&P 500 (monthly index) tends to peak 6.5 months, on average, before the economy peaks and falls into a recession. The S&P 500 (monthly index) tends to hit its trough 4.1 months, on average, before the economy hits its trough and the expansion begins.[6] You can observe some modest dipping during recessionary periods and rises through expansions. The most obvious fluctuation? Look how the S&P 500 took off beginning in the early 1990s. You can see easily how the stock market over a decade appreciated in value.

Chart 7-2

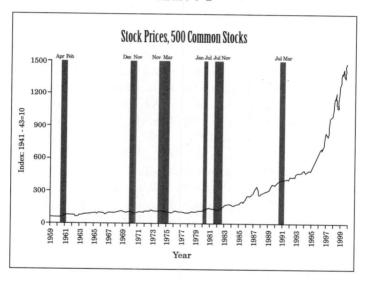

Summary

The S&P 500 is a market-weighted stock indicator. The composite is followed by investment managers for its widespread coverage of top investment-grade stocks and its spectacular returns.

Characteristically, the S&P 500 hits its high point a few months before the economy enters a recession and falls off during the recession. Investors are selling and this pushes stock prices downward. But this is when you want to be buying—at a downtime for the market. If the S&P 500 is down, it is likely the stocks you are interested in are down as well. A few months before the economy picks up and enters an expansion, the S&P 500 starts moving upward. During an expansion, investors see the economy favorably and buy stocks. Forceful buying puts upward pressure on the price of stocks. Now is your time to sell. Watching the S&P 500 can help you benefit from your stock investments.

Tracking S&P 500

Check out the S&P 500 to plan all of your stock-related moves.

Frequency: The indicator is released on a daily basis. Check the number frequently during the month, for at least one month, to get a feel for the trend.

When: Changes are posted throughout the day, but the closing S&P 500 number is the number most widely reported.

Where: It is frequently found on local and national television programs. CNNfn gives wide coverage to this indicator. Look it up in most business sections of any local, regional, or national newspaper. You can catch it daily in national circulation newspapers such as the *New York Times,* the *Washington Post,* or *USA Today.* Check it out in a regional publication such as the *Miami Herald,* the *Los Angeles Times,* the *San Jose Mercury News,* the *Chicago Tribune,* the *Oregonian,* the *Tampa Tribune,* the *Houston Chronicle,* and Louisville's *Courier-Journal.* Both *The Wall Street Journal* and *Investor's Business Daily* list the S&P 500 on the front page, with more details found inside the paper. You can also call (800) 592-6051 for information on the index.

How: The data is released as a number such as 1479.85. Pay particular attention to the news stories that discuss the current strength or weakness of the S&P 500.

Use the following chart to track S&P 500:

S & P 500

January	
February	
March	
April	
May	
June	
July	
August	
September	
October	
November	
December	

Notes on Trend:

Chapter 8

Easy or Tight?
M2 Money Supply

"Money is power, freedom, a cushion, the root of all evil, the sum of blessings."

—Carl Sandburg

Chances are you will get some type of loan—car, home, boat, or install-ment—over the next few years; or you might be in the market to refi-nance your mortgage or pay off high-interest credit cards with a lower-interest home equity loan. Watch M2 money supply on a regular monthly basis so that when you are ready to secure your loan, you have a track record of monetary fluctuations to help you make wise credit choices.

The United States has approximately $4.5 trillion in money supply. There are actually three types of money classified by the Federal Reserve. We are going to be monitoring only one of them, M2, because of its predictable track record. The components of M2 include the follow-ing: coin, currency, checkable deposits (checking accounts, credit union share draft accounts, and NOW accounts), travelers checks, savings deposits, money market deposit accounts, small-denomination time deposits (less than $100,000 including retail repurchase liabilities), and retail money market mutual funds. Its movements provide indications of both recessions and expansions. M2 has such a strong record that it is a part of the LEI.

We are keenly interested in watching money supply because it is a measure of liquidity for the economy. Banking institutions make loans using your savings deposits, checking deposits, time deposits, money market accounts, and more. During a recession, the level of money supply falls and banking institutions are not generously extending loans—car, installment, mortgage, or commercial. You can still get a loan, but it is tougher and you may need to try some alternative lending sources. On the other hand, during an expansion the level of money supply rises. The economy is liquid, lenders are furiously making loans, and credit is easier to obtain. Look to M2 money supply to give you direction on where to look for the best loan, how to determine whether you can handle another loan, and what is the best timing for credit moves.

Where to Find M2 Money Supply

Every Thursday, the Federal Reserve releases the weekly and monthly figures (with updates) for the monetary aggregates. While the weekly figures are often erratic, the monthly monetary data exhibit low volatility. Alternatively, you can check out the seasonally adjusted M2 monthly money supply figure. And for viewing peaks and troughs, monthly monetary data adjusted for inflation is even better. The first monthly figure is released near the middle of the month that follows the data month, but it is not widely covered by the popular press and media. Most papers cover the numbers only as news merits. You will likely need to go to Friday's edition of *The Wall Street Journal* (in the Federal Reserve Data section) or *Investor's Business Daily* (in the Economic Briefs section). Call (212) 339-0330 for a recorded message listing M2 inflation-adjusted data for the most recent three months available.

To get a feel for credit availability, check out the M2 number for at least three months.

What the Number Says

Besides watching in envy as the dollar amount of money grows, or feeling the pain as the number falls, you can watch the total amount of credit availability for hints. Specifically, the level of M2 (adjusted for inflation) hits its high point roughly one year, on average, before the economy enters a recession. M2 will decline through the downtimes. During a recession, money is tight and fewer loans are available, which further stifles the economy. Then just three months, on average, before the economy begins to expand, M2 (adjusted for inflation) hits bottom and starts rising. When more money is available for loans, the economy will start to boom—you can jump in and get your loan with ease. M2 falls prior to a recession and declines during the downtimes. You can still get a loan when the level of liquidity is low, but depending on your net worth and credit worthiness you may need to be more resourceful for your financing. You may need to finance through a finance company, retailer, product manufacturer, or use your credit card.

Be cautious: this indicator will tell you about the level of liquidity in the economy, not the level of interest rates. For interest rate hints, see chapter 10 on federal funds and chapter 11 on the interest rate spread for short-term versus long-term rates. Rates are a tricky thing, but you can generally expect higher rates during an expansion. Business is booming and lenders charge increased rates. People and companies want the loans and they will pay the elevated rates. Conversely, expect to see lower rates during a recession. As we will see in the later chapters, the Federal Reserve can raise interest rates by contracting money. Conversely, the Federal Reserve can lower rates by easing up on money. But we are not looking for monetary pinches, we are looking for the widespread rise in money that leads and extends during an expansion, or widespread tightening that leads and continues throughout a recession. So take a peek at money supply to pick up on the economy's liquidity.

Using M2 Money Supply

First and foremost, it is much easier to qualify for credit during an expansion when the level of M2 is high and lenders are more freely extending loans. So knowing the level of M2 and its trend can help you time your credit applications when they are most likely to be looked on favorably. However, lenders may still be willing to evaluate your credit application when M2 is down and the country is in a liquidity crunch. In fact, if you don't have a stellar credit history, you may be hampered even when M2 is high. Here are a few extra tips to put your credit application in the "accepted" pile.

Lenders typically look at the three C's—character, capacity, and collateral—before extending any type of loan. A character appraisal involves a judgment about a person's willingness to repay bills. Establish a long track record of promptly paying your bills. If you have never taken out a loan before, you likely have no credit history. If you ever find yourself in desperate need of a loan, this lack of credit history can be very detrimental. So take out a small loan, repay it promptly, and build your credit history. But if we are in a tough economic time (money supply will be down) and you are having trouble paying on a current loan, contact your creditor and discuss a repayment plan. This too demonstrates good character because you are acting responsibly and trying to repay.

A capacity appraisal measures your financial capacity to repay debt. Lenders want assurance that you can pay back any new loans that are extended. All of your income will be reviewed: wages, stock dividends, bond income, retirement accounts, and so on. Financial asset income can fluctuate a great deal on a day-to-day basis. But wage income is fairly steady. During an expansion, your job is likely secure. However, in a downtime for the economy, it is essential to show to lenders that you have a secure job. Always stress the stability of your job and your employer. Make notations on your credit application—indicating that you have been the plant supervisor for twenty years can only help you secure your loan. If the company you work for is not a well-known name, jot down a brief statement on its history—for example: "This company is a family-owned manufacturing firm, in operation for thirty-five years." This is just what you want to highlight: stability. The wage factor throws many people out of the loan process during a recession.[1] And to top it off, when M2 is down during a recession, there will be less money available for loans, so the funds will certainly go to the most qualified. Loaning is a competitive business. During a recession, you typically see strong business and personal customers borrowing, so place yourself in that pool.

A capital appraisal evaluates your assets versus your liabilities. Are all of your assets strong enough to pay off existing and potential debt? You must list your financial assets: stocks, bonds, IRAs, insurance policy cash values, savings, and so on. List your physical assets as well: car, house, boat, real estate, and the like. Physical items are not as liquid as financial assets but can be sold to pay off debt, if necessary. If you have overextended your ability to pay back your existing debt easily, you won't be getting a new loan. A credit denial is not the end of the world, however, and does provide an opportunity to plan and reorganize your finances. Once you get your finances back in order you can apply again. If this loan is for something that is a necessity, make an effort to pay down your existing debt and then reapply. Just remember, if your wages and savings are constantly drained to pay off debt, there won't be anything left over for a rainy day. And conversely, just because you qualify doesn't mean that you should take the loan. Think long and hard before signing on the dotted line.

When is the best time to jump in for a loan? It may not be possible to work around the economy when you require a loan, but if the credit is for something that is not a necessity—such as a second home, a boat, or a home improvement—you should definitely time your loan. During an expansion, more money is available and banks are inclined to make loans. If you have great credit, you are more likely to get a loan at any time. When you see the level of M2 start to shoot up, banks will begin granting loans again, but the rates are still likely to be somewhat depressed. This is an optimum time to ask for a loan. So keep your eye on M2. When you see a number of upward movements, beat the competition and make a move to your lending institution.

Which lenders have the lowest rates? The least costly loans are from banks, savings banks, and credit unions. Credit unions, because they are not-for-profit and not subject to taxation, generally offer the lowest rates available. Nevertheless, you must weigh the options available at each particular institution.

The most expensive types of loans are from finance companies, retailers, product manufacturers, and credit cards.[2] Finance companies typically borrow a great deal of their funds from banking institutions. They charge a higher interest rate because they must pay back the bank and still make a profit. Finance companies are likely to lend to people who cannot get credit from a bank, savings bank, or credit union. Because the loans are riskier, you will universally be charged a higher rate.

Retailers such as car dealers, appliance stores, department stores, and product manufacturers also have fairly costly loans with rates that are similar to those charged by finance companies.[3] However, if they really are intent on moving inventory, you may find some spectacular promotional deals with car finance companies, major stores, and big-name product manufacturers. Here, you really need to shop around.

Credit card rates, although an expensive way to finance, have become increasingly competitive over the last few years. Call different companies and ask for their best rate available. If the rates are similar, go for the one with a low or no annual fee.

Always go first for the bank, savings banks, or credit union, regardless of the state of the economy. They will always be comparatively lower. When M2 is down and the economy is in a recession, there is less money to extend. You may need to consider a finance company if you can't get a loan through one of the traditional lenders. One big plus about a finance company is that, because they tend to make smaller loans, your loan is secured much more quickly than it would be with a traditional lender. If you are buying in-store items, you may need to consider going through the retailer. But always evaluate the terms and rates available to you, and compare terms with the product manufacturer to make sure you get the best deal available. Remember to read the fine print, and if you are financing a small purchase, check out different credit card companies for competing rates.

Can you handle another loan? When M2 is up, you will have an easier time getting a loan—but can you afford it? When M2 starts to rise, the economy will pick up shortly. Generally, when the economy is up, so too is the stock market, rates on savings instruments, salary bonuses, sales commissions, and so on. So if the economy is booming, you probably can handle another loan. If you have a secure job and strong financial assets that are prospering, go for it. Be sure to go to a bank, savings bank, or credit union. Some people get hit with the higher finance, retailer, and product manufacturer rates simply because they didn't try elsewhere first.

During a recession many things seem to fall—stock prices dip, savings rates drop, and sales commissions plummet. Financial assets tend to ride the economic cycle. Generally, physical assets—precious metals, art, real estate, boats, cars—tend not to take as intense a beating during a recession. Practically speaking, even though you may qualify for a loan, you certainly don't want to have to sell your physical assets to pay back a loan. If you don't have enough cash to cover the new debt easily, you probably shouldn't consider the loan.

Compilation and Release of the Number

The Federal Reserve employs three different definitions of money—M1, M2, and M3. Can't it just make its mind up which one is right? Actually, they are all right. The Federal Reserve keeps track of the different amounts of money in order to monitor and adjust their growth rates. One of the Federal Reserve's many functions is to oversee monetary policy, seeking to attain a stable and prosperous economy by influencing the money supply and interest rates. This is why there are three levels of money. Here is the breakdown of money as defined by the Federal Reserve:

M1 is the most liquid form of money and includes the types of balances used for daily transactions, including coin and currency, checkable deposits, and travelers checks.

M2 includes M1 plus savings deposits, money market deposit accounts, small-denomination time deposits (less than $100,000 including retail repurchase liabilities), and retail money market mutual funds.

M3 includes M2 plus large-denomination time deposits ($100,000 or more), institutional money market fund balances, repurchase liabilities (overnight and term), and eurodollars (overnight and term).

As you can see, this is a stair-step process, with each higher definition of money being less liquid. The current dollar figure (without deleting for inflation) places M1 at just over $1.1 trillion, and adding the components of savings deposits, money market deposit accounts, small-denomination time deposits, and retail money market mutual funds brings M2 to just over $4.7 trillion. Adding to this large time deposits, institutional money fund balances, overnight and term repurchase liabilities, and eurodollars results in an M3 figure of approximately $6.5 trillion.

The Federal Reserve also has a definition of Debt—the outstanding credit market of the domestic non-financial sectors. This $17.3 trillion includes the U.S. government sector plus the nonfederal sectors (state and local governments, households, nonprofit organizations, non-financial businesses, and farms). Although Debt is not a major instrument of monetary control, the Federal Reserve keys in on examining the debt patterns of households, businesses, and the Federal government.

If the Federal Reserve employs a loose monetary policy, it releases more money into the economy. The money will multiply as banks lend the funds to individuals and businesses, spurring increased output. When there is more money in the economy, it is easier to borrow. When the Federal Reserve decides on a tight monetary policy, the amount of money in the economy shrinks. Tight money results in fewer loans and curtailed economic activity. As the Federal Reserve adjusts the money supply, it constantly monitors the levels of the monetary aggregates and Debt to make sure they are growing or shrinking as the Federal Reserve wishes.

For a publication jam-packed with monetary data and text—including the Federal Reserve Chair's Statement to Congress, Minutes of the FOMC, and other vital Federal Reserve announcements, consult the *Federal Reserve Bulletin*. It is published by the Board of Governors of the Federal Reserve System and can be obtained from Publication Services, Mail Stop 127, Board of Governors of the Federal Reserve System, Washington, D.C. 20051. The price is $25 a year. It may also be purchased by calling (202) 452-3244 or 3245.

Historically, M2 (adjusted for inflation) starts to dip one year prior to a recession and falls during the recession. On average, around three months prior to an expansion, M2 picks up. It will rise fast and furiously during the expansion. The current expansion began in April 1991. In November 1990, M2 hit bottom and picked up from there. The ride upward has not stopped as of this writing. For example, in November 1990 money supply hit a low point of $3,410.5 billion and has kept right on moving up. The level for December 1990 was 3,414.5 billion, January 1991 was $3,416.2 billion, February 1991 was $3,430.9 billion, March 1991 was $3,447.8 billion, and April 1991 was $3,451.3 billion. Certainly, there have been monthly dips here and there, but the ride has been upward. You can see the M2 totals for one year listed in Chart 8-1.

Chart 8-1

M2 Money Supply
(in billions, 1996 dollars)

July 1999	4,341.8
August 1999	4,351.2
September 1999	4,354.9
October 1999	4,364.0
November 1999	4,380.7
December 1999	4,400.2
January 2000	4,410.3
February 2000	4,401.3
March 2000	4,416.9
April 2000	4,453.4
May 2000	4,448.9
June 2000	4,448.1

Source: Business Cycle Indicators

The largely upward rise is consistent with an expansion. What you want to be looking for is a noticeable change or dip. At the beginning of the last recession, money supply started to fall around seven months prior. So be cautious of any noticeable dips in the numbers. If it starts to fall from its mid-$4 trillion range, you should grow very cautious of tough times ahead.

If You Want to Know More: The Federal Reserve

The Federal Reserve is the central bank of the United States. It was founded by Congress in 1913 to provide the country with a safe, flexible, and stable monetary and financial system. Besides conducting monetary policy and maintaining stability of the financial system, the Federal Reserve supervises and regulates banking institutions. The Federal Reserve protects the credit rights of consumers and provides select financial services to the government, public financial institutions, and even foreign official institutions.

Money and Inflation

Here's the deal. When money expands too rapidly, people are able to spend money more easily. Guess what rears its ugly head? You guessed it—inflation. On the flip side, if money does not grow quickly enough, the economy will grow stagnant. We need enough money for spending to result in a prosperous economy, but not so much money that prices rise and send us into an inflationary spiral. Implementing monetary policy is somewhat like walking a tightrope.

If the Federal Reserve ever becomes concerned that we are spending too much, so much so that inflation is a looming threat, it attempts a tight monetary policy. Less money in the economy increases loan competition and interest rates rise. We spend less, resulting in declining inflation.

Some economists watch current M2 as an indicator of upcoming inflation. But this relationship is tricky. Here's the thinking: if money supply is increased, people will spend more and output will rise. Will this lead to higher prices? Maybe or maybe not. If we are below full employment (as you recall from chapter 4, full employment is defined as 94 percent employment), most of the increases in money will simply translate into increased production. If we are fully employed, an increase in money will likely lead to an increase in prices. Money moves the economy, and we need it to survive in a sophisticated economy. But figuring the complicated effects of its ups and downs is what the Federal Reserve struggles with on a daily basis.

> No dollar bill higher than $100 has been printed since 1945. And in 1969 all bills over $100 were removed from circulation as they were turned in to the Federal Reserve. Gone is the $500 William McKinley, the $1,000 Grover Cleveland, the $5,000 James Madison, and the $10,000 Salmon P. Chase.

Business Cycle Activity

M2 (in inflation-adjusted dollars) peaks about 12.5 months before the economy does. In other words, M2 starts its decline about a year before the economy starts its fall. This stands to reason—as less money is available, fewer loans are made, and business activity ultimately slacks off. M2 bottoms out and starts to rise 3.2 months before the economy hits bottom.[4] As money starts to pick up, more loans will be made and business will start to boom. You can see the dips during recessionary periods and the increases during expansions.

Chart 8-2

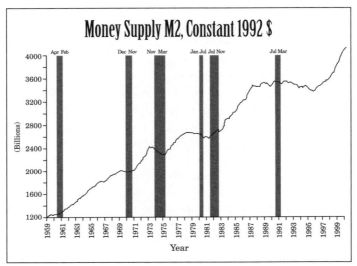

Money Supply M2, Constant 1992 $

Financial Participants' Reaction

The monetary aggregates have a following, particularly among economists. But the stock and bond market players are keyed into the words of Federal Reserve officials. They particularly listen to all the Federal Reserve chairman's speeches and testimonies. C-Span is a great place to watch many of the proceedings live. Twice a year, in February and June, the chairman of the Federal Reserve reports to Congress at hearings on monetary policy (see the Federal Reserve Testimony and Speeches website, www.bog.frb.fed.us/s-t.htm, for testimonies and speeches of Federal Reserve Board officials).

Who can forget the famous "irrational exuberance" speech in 1996? Years later, it is still widely referenced. Giving a speech at the American Enterprise Institute for Public Policy Research (a well-respected Washington, D.C., think tank), Federal Reserve Chairman Alan Greenspan posed two questions. He asked, "How do we know when irrational exuberance has unduly escalated asset values…And how do we factor that assessment into monetary policy?"[5]

U.S. markets were closed at the time of the speech, but word of his speech spread. Did the Federal Reserve chairman want to send a subtle hint to the stock market? Maybe. When the market opened, the Dow lost nearly 145.35 points within the first half-hour. Traders were concerned the chairman of the Federal Reserve was essentially saying that stock and bond prices were overvalued and that money supply would be tightened to force rates up. The market soon calmed, and the Dow closed the day down just 55.16 points. So rather than watching monetary data, the market watches what the Federal Reserve deems best for a strong economy.

Summary

The monetary figure, M2 (in inflation-adjusted dollars) leads the economy's peaks and troughs. Movements in M2 lead the economy's highs and lows. It is vital to watch money supply because it is a measure of liquidity for our economy. During a recession, the level of money supply falls and banking institutions are not busy extending loans. M2 is the indicator to watch for everything related to loans and financing. If you have excellent credit, you should have no trouble getting a loan or refinancing your mortgage. An added plus is that rates are universally down during a recession. But it is tougher to get credit so you may need to try a finance company, retailer, product manufacturer, or use your credit card. Be sure to shop around for the best rates. When the level of money supply rises, soon we will be in an expansion. The economy is liquid, business is booming, and lenders are furiously making loans. Credit will be easier to obtain, but make sure you can afford it before you sign up for a new loan.

Tracking M2 Money Supply

Check out the M2 number to get a feel for credit availability.

Frequency: The indicator is released on a monthly basis. To get a feel for credit availability, track the M2 number for at least three months.

When: Every Thursday the Federal Reserve releases the weekly and monthly figures (with updates) for the monetary aggregates. While the weekly figures are often erratic, the monthly monetary data exhibits low volatility. The first monthly figure is released near the middle of the month following the month being covered.

Where: This indicator is not widely covered by the popular press and media. Most papers cover the number only as news merits. Most likely, you will need to check out Friday's edition of *The Wall Street Journal* (in the Federal Reserve Data section) or *Investor's Business Daily* (in the Economic Briefs section). Be sure to note the seasonally adjusted M2 monthly money supply figure. For viewing peaks and troughs, monthly monetary data adjusted for inflation is even better. You can call (212) 339-0330 for a recorded message that lists M2 inflation-adjusted data for the most recent three months available.

How: The data is released as a large dollar amount, such as $4,453.9 billion. It is likely that you won't find commentary on this specific monetary indicator. However, you will see news stories on the Federal Reserve's general easing or contracting of money supply, which will give you a clue on the upcoming general direction of M2.

Use the following chart to track M2 Money Supply:

M2 Money Supply

January	
February	
March	
April	
May	
June	
July	
August	
September	
October	
November	
December	

Notes on Trend:

Chapter 9

Is It a Good Time to Open a Business?
Corporate Profits after Tax

"The smell of profit is clean and sweet, whatever the source."
—Juvenal

The Gap Inc. and Cisco Systems Inc. both recently reported strong corporate profits—a good deal for the stockholders. But if you don't own stock in the clothing mega-giant or the Internet networking king, why should you care? You should care because corporate profits, essentially a firm's income over expenses, is an important indicator of the future overall health of the economy. If the profits of these corporate firms are strong, it is a good sign of prosperous times for all. And if you have been thinking about opening a business of your own, look to corporate profitability to help find the perfect opportunity.

Corporate Profits After Tax leads both recessions and expansions. What is the reasoning? When Corporate Profits After Tax are strong, companies will have the funds to expand plants, build new stores, introduce new products, and hire more employees. Thinking about opening a business? Jump in when profits are high, which means that companies and individuals will be able to buy your service or product. On the other hand, if Corporate Profits After Tax is a depressed figure, guess what will happen? Due to financial necessity and uncertainty about the business climate, firms will scrap expansion plans, postpone the introduction of new lines, and let people go. Hold off on starting up that dream business until times are better. When corporate profits are down, it's a telltale sign that business times are tough. Due to depressed profitability, however, you may just find an existing business that is for sale that you just can't pass up. The great bargain price may make it worth your while to get going with your business.

> The familiar Gap opened 570 new stores in fiscal 1999, with 299 of these stores located in the United States. At the end of the year, the company had a total of 3,018 stores, with 1,767 in the United States. Gap reported net earnings of $1.127 billion for the year, a whopping 37 percent increase compared to $825 million for 1998. Guess all that advertising pays off!

Where to Find Corporate Profits After Tax

Corporate Profits After Tax is a quarterly figure. It is first released (along with GDP data) late in the second month after the close of the quarter. Quarter one is released in late May, quarter two in late August, and quarter three in late November. Late in the third month after the quarter ends, a final revision is published, so jot it down if you get the chance. All quarters, except for quarter four, which has a preliminary and final estimate published in late March of the following year, have a preliminary and final release. Some national television news programs report on the quarterly number, particularly if the change is notable. On television, you generally can catch the figure on the day of or the day after its release. The day after its release, it is covered in newspaper publications running the story. Big newspapers like the *New York Times* cover the Corporate Profits After Tax, and the *Washington Post* reports on the number as news merits. The trend of many regional newspapers is to cover the figure only if it is big news.

If you miss the news coverage, on the day following the release you can get the number in *The Wall Street Journal* (in the Economy section). You can catch it in *Investor's Business Daily*, but it is run at the editor's discretion, so you are likely to see it only if it is particularly high or low. You can also call (202) 606-5306 to get the information from a recorded message.

To get a feel for small business opportunities, watch the number for at least three quarters in order to track a trend.

What the Number Says

The profit data represents all incorporated firms in the United States, both publicly traded and privately owned. There are roughly five million corporate tax returns filed each year. Corporate America is big business; the total annual Corporate Profits After Tax figure reaches approximately $650 billion.

The number for Corporate Profits After Tax is released every quarter (every three months). When the figure rises, it is an indication that big business is booming. Just two quarters, on average, prior to the economy's expansion, the figure will hit bottom and start to rise. It will rise (excluding some dips here and there) throughout the expansion. Take the clue from existing firms and get into the business environment when the getting is good. But four quarters prior to a recession, on average, the number will peak and slide downward throughout the depressed period. The lower figure suggests it is a challenging time to open most new businesses. There are notable exceptions: due to failing corporate profitability, you may find an existing business for sale at a steal. And if you are looking for a winner, you can always find businesses that operate very strongly, even during a recession. Look to a business where people are always spending regardless of the economy—like health-related firms, food and drink enterprises, and clothing and personal care businesses. So let's take a look at how this one simple number can help make you profitable.

Using Corporate Profits After Tax

Maybe you are thinking big. You are contemplating quitting your job and diving into small business ownership, and opening a store at the mall, local outlet, or industrial section of town. Or perhaps you have been thinking about a side business you could run from your home. Regardless, any size business is a big venture. There are so many questions to answer. What type of business? When to start operations? Should you go with a new start-up or buy an existing business? What about a franchise? Look to corporate America for your clue in starting up or buying a business. If you want your venture to be profitable, there is no better indicator to watch than Corporate Profits After Tax.

When is the best time to start a new business? Interpreting this indicator is simple. When you see profits start to consistently move up, you have your clue. Because this indicator is published quarterly, make sure you have at least three quarters of figures before you make a move. It is only measured every three months and can easily have an off quarter. Because Profits is not a frequent measurement, don't jump to any quick conclusions. In addition, remember you can always complement your reading of profits with the other indicators to make sure you are right on track. If Corporate Profits After Tax is down, it is going to be tough opening a new business. It will be very challenging to make money when big business is not doing well. So play it safe. Watch the number and when it is down, hold off on small business ownership. And with a recession, you likely will have ample warning (the length of a recession warning will vary, however). On average, Corporate Profits After Tax falls four quarters—one whole year—prior to a recession.

Do you need tips on buying an existing business? If you choose to buy an ongoing business, you may just find some steals on existing businesses for sale. Due to decreased corporate profitability, the classified pages will be full of companies for sale, some at great bargain prices. Realizing that the business environment is against you and the economy is tough, you may still find some opportunities that you just shouldn't pass by. A bargain price coupled with your fresh innovative ideas and entrepreneurship may turn a newly acquired slipping venture into a booming business If you feel you can succeed in a depressed economy, or even coast until the economy edges out of the recession, or if you are contemplating a business in an industry that is recession-proof—health care or entertainment, to name two—this may be an excellent time to make a deal.

Are there any hints that a firm for sale will be profitable in the long term? Regardless of the state of the economy, there are some questions that you can pose to the selling party that may give you a hint of continued profitability for the firm. First and foremost, attempt to find out why the owner is selling now. If the owner is selling during a recession, you must strongly suspect profitability trouble. Can you address this and still make it worth your while? During an expansion, or strong profits, you must still examine the financial ratios to investigate individual profitability. Is the owner selling because she wants to retire? If so, she may simply want out of the rat race. The owner may not be overly concerned about price as long as she makes a decent profit. Here, you may have stumbled upon a spectacular deal. Is this person in the business of buying and selling companies? If so, it doesn't matter about what is going on in the economy—no deals here. Ask questions to discover more about the true operations and likely long-term profitability of the firm. Following are a few questions to get you started:

- When did the owner start the company? Is he the original owner? (Too many owners is a big red flag that this business is not going to be a profit-maker—otherwise individuals would have stayed longer.)

- Has the company ever been involved in any lawsuits? If so, where do they stand? (Depending on the type of litigation this could be a sign of trouble for you. Legal fees can drain profitability, so you want to stay away from them.)

☞ Who runs the company? Do you need a manager and employees? How long have the employees been at the firm? (If this company has long-term employees whom you can retain, it is a big plus. Employees can make or break the business.)

☞ Who are the company's customers—businesses, individuals, government, or a mix? (Government customers, due to the availability of funds, are highly stable buyers though there often is a large lag time for you to receive payment. Business customers tend to be fairly stable. Individuals tend to be less stable, and their buying patterns move with the economy. Knowing the customer base will give you a hint about future reliability of purchases.)

☞ What is the sales history? Are the sales fairly level all year or are customer purchases seasonal? (If available, take a peek at how the business has weathered over the years through recessions and expansions. This will give you a hint of profitability patterns in the future.)

What about starting a new business when corporate profitability is down? If you want to start a business when corporate profits are down, you can still succeed. You may have a necessity business or a recession-proof idea that will boom. Ask yourself, what businesses make money when others are not profitable and the economy is down? Look to a business where people are always spending regardless of the economy, such as health-related firms, food and drink enterprises, and clothing and personal-care businesses. Certainly, there are others sectors, and depending where you open your business, the answers may vary. You must have a feel for the type of customers you will be serving. What will they spend their money on? What is important to them? The necessity firms won't experience the highs of the luxury firms, but the companies tend to stay more stable over the business cycle. Keep your mind open and evaluate all reasonable opportunities. And don't get too anxious. Remember, the average recession lasts just under a year, so bad times continue only so long. The best strategy may be to use your time wisely and plan for your new venture during a better economic cycle. Times will be booming soon.

Compilation and Release of the Number

Corporate Profit After Tax includes the net current-production income of organizations treated as corporations in the BEA's National Income Product Accounts. Corporations are defined by the BEA as follows: "organizations consist[ing] of all entities required to file Federal corporate tax returns, including mutual financial institutions and cooperatives subject to Federal income tax; private noninsured pension funds; nonprofit institutions that primarily serve business; Federal Reserve banks; and federally sponsored credit agencies."[1] The profit figures include all incorporated U.S. businesses, both private and public corporations.

The Conference Board has identified both Corporate Profits After Tax and Corporate Profits After Tax (in constant dollars) as leading indicators at both peaks and troughs. (The constant dollar component is adjusted for the effects of inflation.) These figures are available from Business Cycle Indicators and are an economist favorite because they are consistent with adjusted GDP growth. But either indicator will do the trick as long as you are consistent in looking at the same figure each quarter.

Chart 9-1

Corporate Profits News Releases

Subject	Approximate Timing of Release
(January/February/March) First Quarter (Preliminary)	Late May
(January/February/March) First Quarter (Revised)	Late June
(April/May/June) Second Quarter (Preliminary)	Late August
(April/May/June) Second Quarter (Revised)	Late September
(July/August/September) Third Quarter (Preliminary)	Late November
(July/August/September) Third Quarter (Revised)	Late December
(October/November/December) Fourth Quarter (Final)	Late March

The data is released along with a drove of GDP data, late in the second month after the close of the quarter. Late in the third month, after the quarter ends, they publish a final revision. All quarters have both a preliminary release and a final release for corporate profits, except the fourth quarter. The first and final estimates for fourth quarter corporate profits are published in late March. The preliminary and the final quarterly figures can differ a bit, so chart both, if possible, and rely on the final for trends. Chart 9-1 lists the approximate times of the Corporate Profits News Release Dates. All are released at 8:30 A.M. Eastern Time. As the dates approach, because it is released with the GDP, the financial publications widely publicize the exact date of the upcoming release.

The first quarter 2000 (revised) press release listed the following Corporate Profits After Tax figures:

Profits after tax increased $35.2 billion, compared with an increase of $16.3 billion [in the fourth quarter]. Dividends increased $6.5 billion, compared with an increase of $6.2 billion; undistributed profits increased $28.7 billion, compared with an increase of $10.1 billion.[2]

Corporate Profits: Level
(Billions of Dollars)
Seasonally adjusted at annual rates

	Profits after tax	Dividends	Undistributed Profits
I 1999	570.1	356.4	213.7
II 1999	581.4	361.5	219.9
III 1999	594.3	367.3	227.0
IV 1999	610.6	373.5	237.1
I 2000	645.8	380.0	265.8

Source: U.S. Department of Commerce Bureau of the Economic Analysis

Profits after tax are profits after firms have paid taxes but before they have paid dividends.[3] The figure technically consists of dividends and undistributed corporate profits. Dividends are simply a distribution of the profits of the company to its shareholders. You can glean from the chart that profits before dividends fluctuate more than the dividends.

Common stock dividend payments are at the discretion of the firms' board of directors and can fluctuate based on economic conditions, but many companies tend to keep common stock dividend payments fairly constant. The remaining figure, undistributed profits, is often referred to as retained earnings, serving to increase the value of the firm to shareholders and adding to financial reserves.

You can see that the trend of increasing corporate profits is consistent with a strong economy. Back in April 1991 when the country began its expansion, corporate profits were under the $300 billion level. It has risen to nearly $650 billion and is still going strong. What you want to keep your eye open for is a notable dip that would suggest a recession.

If You Want to Know More: The Bureau of Economic Analysis (BEA)

Every quarter, the BEA of the Department of Commerce releases extensive corporate profit figures, including profits from current production, domestic profits, the foreign component of profits, and profits before tax, among others. We are specifically interested in the after-tax profits of corporate enterprises. The data is only available quarterly because the information is collected largely from the companies' annual reports. The most recent year's data are profits from the Census Bureau's quarterly survey of corporate profits, regulator agency reports and compilations of publicly available corporate financial statements. Other years are taken from the IRS's tabulation of business tax returns, adjusted for understatement of income on tax returns and for conceptual differences.[4] Because the BEA uses the individual company's tax books (versus a company's financial books), conceptual differences, such as excluding capital gain and loss income, or not recognizing bad debt losses as current expenses, will cause differences between the BEA figures and the numbers in the company's financial reports.[5] The BEA typically conducts an annual revision each July, revising the prior three years' estimates. Benchmark revisions occur about every five years.

The BEA's mission is to produce and disseminate timely, relevant, and cost-effective economic accounts statistics that provide a comprehensive, up-to-date picture of economic activity.[6] As an agency of the Department of Commerce, the BEA produces a wide variety of national, regional, and international quantitative estimates. The most widely recognized national economic accounts deal with GDP and its components. Examples of regional data include state personal income and gross state product. International data includes U.S. international trade in goods and services, and U.S. foreign direct investment in the United States.

Chart 9-2

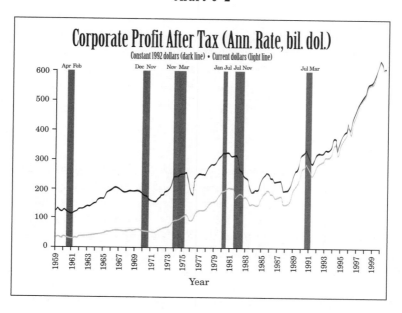

Corporate Profit After Tax (Ann. Rate, bil. dol.)
Constant 1992 dollars (dark line) • Current dollars (light line)

Business Cycle Activity

As you can see from the chart, corporate profits (both corporate profits after tax and constant dollars) tend to fall before a recession and pick up before an expansion. You can see the decline during the recession years. Conversely, you can see the rise in profits during the expansionary periods. Corporate Profits After Tax peaks, on average, roughly four quarters ahead of the economy's peaks. Corporate Profits After Tax hits bottom, on average, around two quarters prior to the economy's troughs. You can easily observe the decline in Corporate Profits After Tax during the recessionary phases and an upward, although volatile, increase during the expansions.

Cisco Systems, Inc. is a world leader in networking for the Internet. Founded in 1984 by a small group of computer scientists from Stanford University, the company shipped its first product in 1986. Today the firm has more than 20,000 employees in fifty-five countries. For Cisco's 1999 fiscal year, the Internet company reported net income for the year of $2.10 billion, compared with fiscal 1998 net income of $1.35. Now how's that for growth?

Financial Participants' Reaction

Financial players do not typically react to the BEA's release of Corporate Profits, primarily because of its delayed release. Individual quarterly reports of big companies have already been released by the time the BEA issues its numbers, so the market already has a rough idea of whether it is a strong or a weak business environment for corporate firms.

Summary

Corporate Profits After Tax is a quick and easy indicator to watch. Released quarterly, profits are directly tied to the economy. Strong profits give businesses the opportunity and confidence to expand business activities, further boosting the economy. If you are interested in starting a business for yourself, get in on the profitability opportunities and start operations. But watch corporate profits fall, and businesses will pull back on production, expansion, and hiring. Times are tough for the corporate community, so hold off on your business venture. Low corporate profits are a sign that it is going to be tough to survive in a new venture, but it may be a good time to buy an existing business. The corporate sector is a mover and shaker of our economy, and this profitability indicator provides an unparalleled peek into the overall health of the economy in the coming months.

Tracking Corporate Profits After Tax

Check out Corporate Profits After Tax to get hints about the profitability of opening your own small business:

Frequency: The indicator is released on a quarterly basis. To get a feel for small business opportunities, watch the number for at least three quarters and track the trend.

When: It is first released (along with GDP data) late in the second month after the close of the quarter. Quarter one is released in late May, quarter two in late August, and quarter three in late November. Late in the third month after the quarter ends, a final revision is published, which you also should jot down if you hear it. There is a preliminary and final release for all of the quarters except for quarter four, which has a first and final estimate published in late March of the following year.

Where: Some national television news programs report on the quarterly number, particularly if the change was notable. You can catch the number usually on the day of or the day after its release on television. Often, it is covered in newspaper publications running the story. Widely circulated newspapers such as the *New York Times* cover it, and the *Washington Post* reports on the number as news merits. The trend of many regional newspapers is to cover the figure if it is big news. If you miss it on the news, catch it in *The Wall Street Journal* (in the Economy section) on the day following the release. You may find it in *Investor's Business Daily,* but it is run at the editor's discretion so you are likely to see it only if it is particularly high or low. You can also call a recorded message at (202) 606-5306.

How: The press and television news may report the quarterly increase or decrease in Corporate Profits from one quarter to the next with such statements as, "Profits after tax of U.S. corporations increased $14.9 billion for quarter two, compared to an increase of $34.5 billion for the previous quarter." You may also find the rate of change from the previous quarter reported: "After tax profits of U.S. corporations rose 2.4 percent in quarter two compared with a 5.7 percent rise the previous quarter." Look for commentary with the numbers like "spectacular growth" or "a down quarter for corporate profitability."

Use the following chart to track Corporate Profits After Tax:

Corporate Profits After Tax

Q1: Jan/Feb/Mar	
Q2: Apr/May/Jun	
Q3: Jul/Aug/Sep	
Q4: Oct/Nov/Dec	

Notes on Trend:

Chapter 10

An Early Warning Signal: Federal Funds Rate

"Change is the law of life. And those who look to the past or present are certain to miss the future."

—John F. Kennedy

Wouldn't it be nice to have a substantial hint on which way interest rates were going? You can with federal funds. Bond players watch federal funds for directional changes. When interest rates go up, bond prices fall, so you can jump in the bond market and buy low. When interest rates go down, bond prices rise, so now is the time to sell. This one key interest rate will give you great buy-and-sell early warning signals that will allow you to profit in the bond market. Further, it is the first interest rate to turn down prior to a recession and the only interest rate that acts as a leading indicator for foretelling recessions. In addition, almost all short-term interest rates are based on the level of federal funds. So any decisions you are making that are affected by interest rates—borrowing, refinancing, investing—can be better informed if you are watching this indicator.

You are going to react to interest rate shifts, and you may trade on temporary glitches up or down in rates. Nevertheless, you should check the rate for at least one month, simply to identify upward or downward patterns that indicate how interest rates are moving.

Where to Find the Federal Funds Rate

The Federal Funds Rate is covered on national and local television programs and is published in most newspapers. CNNfn gives widespread coverage to this number. It is particularly big news on the day the Federal Reserve meets to consider changing interest rates, which happens about every six weeks. You can find the number on a regular basis in such newspapers as the *New York Times,* the *Washington Post,* the *Miami Herald,* the *Tampa Tribune,* the *Los Angeles Times,* the *Chicago Tribune,* the *Oregonian,* the *Houston Chronicle*, and the *San Jose Mercury News* (in Saturday's Business section). Plus, many local newspapers run the number. *USA Today* covers every Federal Reserve meeting and reports the number even when it doesn't change.

In addition, you can always locate the number each and every day in the Money Rates Sections of both *The Wall Street Journal* and *Investor's Business Daily.* For consistency, track the last bid rate of the day.

If you are investing in bonds, you don't need a long historical track record. You can immediately tell the direction of rates and their effect on bond prices. Simply check the figure frequently for the month before you actually invest.

What the Number Says

Federal funds are overnight loans between banking institutions. The interest rate paid on these loans is called the federal funds rate. These are temporary excess reserves loaned by one bank to another. The term "federal funds" arose because the loans are made with balances that the banking institutions keep with the Federal Reserve. The Federal Reserve, acting as a go-between in the transaction, simply moves funds from one banking account to another. The majority of these transactions are overnight loans from banking institutions that have extra reserves at the end of the day lending to institutions short on their reserve balances.[1] Required reserves on checkable deposits (checking accounts, credit union share draft accounts, and NOW accounts) must be held in the form of deposits with the Federal Reserve (or in the bank's vault cash). No interest is ever paid on reserves so banking institutions tend to keep the actual level of reserves close to the amount required by law.

For bond traders, a rise in the Federal Funds Rate is a good sign because it signals a great opportunity. When interest rates rise, bond prices fall. If you want to make money in the bond market, buy when bond prices are depressed. When interest rates go down, the price of bonds will go up. Here is your sell signal. Many experienced traders watch the federal funds for a signal on the direction of interest rates.

If the Federal Reserve feels that money is too available in the economy, it can pull money out of the banking system by selling government securities to bank institutions. Banks pay for the investment, money is reduced in the banking system, and the Federal Funds Rate is pushed up. Conversely, if the economy needs stimulating, the Federal Reserve will buy government securities from banking institutions, thus increasing the level of money in the economy. This increased availability of money, which eases borrowing, reduces the level on interest rates, specifically the Federal Funds Rate.

Stock players and bond players are highly tuned in to the Federal Reserve's movements on interest rates. While affecting both participants, interest rates are an extremely important factor for the bond market. Bond prices reflect changes in market conditions. Remember, interest rates and bond prices are inversely related. Here's why. Bonds are sold with a stated interest rate. That means they will pay you the same amount every six months, regardless of what is going on in the economy. What does fluctuate is the bond price, the amount the bond is selling for on the secondary market. And the price of bonds is affected highly by interest rates.

Unlike stocks, bonds have a maturity (payment due date). Bonds typically sell for face value, generally $1,000 or $5,000, and have common maturities of five, ten, fifteen, twenty, or thirty years. When the bond matures, you will receive your original principal payment, regardless of how the bond fluctuated since it was issued. Let's just say you have an old bond paying 8 percent interest. You would get paid $80 a year (or $40 every six months) for each $1,000 investment in a bond. If interest rates go up, new comparable bonds would be paying a higher rate and the price of your bond would fall. Let's say rates on new bonds of similar quality and maturity are now earning 9 percent. Those bond-holders would be getting $90 in interest each year. Your bond is not looking so attractive now. The price of your bond will fall in the secondary market to compensate for the lower interest rate. Say instead that interest rates fell and new similar bonds are issued at a 7 percent rate. A holder of the new bond would receive only $70 a year. Now your bond is looking pretty good with that higher interest payment. People would want your bond, and its price would rise.

Certainly, there are other factors that affect bond prices: the maturity of the bond, the quality of the instrument, the strength of the issuing company, and the direction of long-term rates. However, because the Federal Funds Rate is controlled by the Federal Reserve and does predict the direction of short-term rates, it is watched closely by the bond market. A strict tightening of credit by the Federal Reserve can force short-term rates higher than long-term rates while easing of the money supply generally allows short-term rates to decline compared to long-term rates. Investor expectations and demand for long or short-term rates can also cause shifts in these rates. So this key short-term rate does provide a general directional strategy for interest rates that bond players tend to watch.

Using the Federal Funds Rate

You can make money in the bond market by buying bonds when interest rates are high (bond prices are down) and selling bonds when rates are down (when bond prices are up). Looking to federal funds can provide a general direction for buying and selling in the bond market. Along with some good old common sense, federal funds can provide investment direction for your bond portfolio.

There are many reasons why bonds are generally considered a safer investment than stocks. When you invest in a corporate or government bond you are actually loaning money to the issuer of the bond for a set period of time, in return for a set interest payment. You can buy bonds through a broker, or directly from the government if it is a Treasury issue. The interest payments generally come every six months. When the bond matures, you will get your principal investment back. So regardless of how the price of the bond fluctuated after it was issued, you will get the principal back upon maturity. As a bond-holder, you are a lender to the issuer, and the company must pay you before it can pay a dividend to shareholders. Stockholders are long-term owners of a company. All of their investment is at risk. Of course, you can trade this bond before it matures. Due to the demand and supply of bonds in the secondary market, bond prices fluctuate prior to maturity.

You can do well with investments by trading bonds actively, and you will have to watch the Federal Funds Rate. When rates move down, bond prices will fall. Watch the Federal Funds Rate for its movement. Generally speaking, when the Federal Reserve starts to shift rates, it will be for a significant time period, to accomplish a specific objective like damping inflation or spurring economic activity. The Federal Reserve typically does not raise rates and lower rates in a seesaw manner. If you feel that the Federal Funds Rate has hit bottom and bond prices are elevated, it is your time to sell. Conversely, watch the Federal Funds Rate and when rates have been increased and are high, you want to buy, buy, buy because bond prices are down.

With varying maturities of bonds, the decision of which to sell first depends on what's going on with interest rates. Short-term bonds, those bonds that will reach maturity shortly (generally within one year), are not as affected by changes in interest rates as longer-term issues. In your buying strategy be sure to spread your risk by diversifying and purchasing bonds with different maturities—short-term, intermediate, and some long-term issues. Assume you hold a 10 percent bond that is to mature in one year and interest rates universally fall to 9 percent. The price of your bond will no doubt rise because it is offering a very attractive interest payment. But what about the bond-holder who owns a similar 10 percent bond that is to mature in thirty years? The price of that bond is going to shoot way up because it will be paying the elevated interest rate for many more years. On the flip side, assume you are still holding the 10 percent bond and interest rates rise to 11 percent. The price of your bond would not fall too much because you will be getting back $1,000 in just a year and you only suffer through the more modest payments for one year. The other guy will have depressed interest payments for thirty years (assuming the interest rate stays above 10 percent) and the price of his bond is going to plummet.

Along with quality issues, keep in mind the bond's maturity when selling. If you have a long-term bond and interest rates fall, you will be able to make some significant cash. If it is a short-term bond, you can only make spare change. If you are selling, you have more potential for appreciation with a long-term bond but you do also face more risk of capital loss.

If you are convinced that rates are going to go up soon, hold off buying until the rate increase has transpired. Remember, rates and bond prices are inversely related. So if you believe rates are on an upward spiral, postpone buying because bond prices are going to go down even more. Conversely, if you believe that rates have bottomed out, bond prices are elevated so you will want to sell quickly.

You may not have the cash required to obtain a diversified portfolio of bonds. Or perhaps you don't have the time to monitor your investments in the bond market. If not, check out one of the many bond mutual funds. Many require a minimum deposit as low as $1,000. A wide variety of corporate and government bond funds are available. Along with the type and quality of bonds, most specialize in a maturity—short-term, intermediate-term, or long-term bonds. It is a quick and easy way to spread risk because the funds are composed of lots of bonds. Most provide monthly dividend checks because you become part owner of the fund. It has no maturity because as the pool matures the portfolio manager will simply buy more bonds. And bond funds move in the same inverse direction as straight bonds. When interest rates go up, it is a great time to get in the bond mutual fund market as well. When rates fall, the value of your mutual fund rises because the value of the underlying bonds rise, so consider selling.

Compilation and Release of the Number

The buying and selling of government bonds is the Federal Reserve's main monetary policy tool. Follow this abbreviated synopsis of how the Federal Reserve affects the federal funds rate through open market operations. The Federal Reserve buys government bonds in the open market and pays for them by crediting the bank's reserve balance at the Federal Reserve. The banking system now has more money for loans. More loans means more deposits for the banking system and hence more money. As money expands, rates fall. When the Federal Reserve buys bonds, the Federal Funds Rate will fall. What happens if the Federal Reserve sells a bond? When the Federal Reserve sells government bonds in the open market, a banking institution pays for the bonds from their Federal Reserve account. Reserves are reduced, contracting the amount of money available for loans. Fewer loans means interest rates will be pushed up. When the Federal Reserve sells bonds, the Federal Funds Rate will rise.

The actual implementation of open market operations is highly technical, but for illustrative purposes, let's review a concise scenario. Banks must keep reserve requirements (in vault cash or with the Federal Reserve) against their checkable deposits. For this example, assume required reserves to be 10 percent of deposits.[2] Let's assume also that all previous reserve requirements have been met at the banking institutions we are going to visit. Assume further that the Federal Reserve decides to pump new money into the system by buying $10,000 in government bonds in the open market. The Bank of Anytown sold this bond and hence receives the $10,000. Bank of Anytown will keep $1,000 for its reserve balance and lend the other $9,000 to Ms. Smith. Ms. Smith quickly runs to the premier bank in town, Bank of Anystate, and deposits the $9,000 in her checking account. Bank of Anytown keeps $900 to meet its reserve requirement on the money and lends out the other $8,100 to Mr. Jones. Mr. Jones takes the money home, only to be discovered by his wife, Mrs. Jones. She quickly jogs to her bank, Bank of Middletown, and deposits it in her personal checking account. Are you getting the picture? Bank of Middletown needs to keep $810 for its reserve requirement and can lend the remaining $7,190. This scenario could go on and on, which it does throughout the U.S. banking system. Now, this example exaggerates the extent that money will multiply. All the loaned money will not come back to the banking system as a checkable deposit, and some banks may keep a higher reserve ratio than is required by law or may not lend out the full permissible amount.

FOMC Implementation

The Federal Reserve body that implements the daunting task of monetary policy for the United States is the Federal Open Market Committee (FOMC). The organization is composed of the seven members of the Board of Governors of the Federal Reserve Bank (the governing Federal Reserve body) plus five of the twelve Federal Reserve Bank presidents. The Federal Reserve President of New York (that is where open market operations for the Federal Reserve are conducted) is always on the FOMC. The other four members of the FOMC come from the remaining eleven Federal Banks, serving terms based on a rotating schedule. The chair of the Board of Governors, currently Alan Greenspan, is always the chair of the FOMC. All Federal Reserve Bank presidents generally attend the FOMC meetings, but only the official members may vote on actions.

Every six weeks, the Federal Reserve has a monetary policy meeting where it sets target levels for monetary aggregates and the Federal Funds Rate. The meeting dates are widely publicized and are available from the Federal Reserve website. Immediately after each meeting, the Federal Reserve announces the direction and rate adjustment of the Federal Funds Rate if it has decided on a change. There will be an announcement even if the Federal Reserve decides to maintain the same rate. Now here is where you often get a violent reaction from the bond market. If, for example, a rate adjustment was not expected, or it was higher or lower than anticipated, you can get some violent drops or rises in bond prices.

On October 15, 1998, the FOMC called a special meeting to discuss a rate change. The result was a decrease in the rate from 5.25 to 5 percent. And did the market ever react. Here is an excerpt from *The Wall Street Journal* that discusses the federal funds drop and how the bond market reacted:

> The bond market soared after the Federal Reserve announced a surprise cut in the federal-funds rate late in the afternoon.
> While the longest Treasury maturities turned in a strong performance, intermediate bonds did even better.

In late trading, the price of the benchmark 30-year Treasury bond was up $^{31}/_{32}$ point, or \$9.6875 for a bond with a \$1,000 face value, at $108^6/_{32}$. Its yield fell to 4.961% from 5.022% Wednesday, as bond yields move in the opposite direction of prices.[3]

You can read the Federal Reserve minutes, published on the website two days after the next meeting, to glean further hints about the direction of interest rates. Generally, the Federal Reserve is fairly consistent in its raising or lowering of rates. It doesn't move back and forth indiscriminately. Generally, if it is raising or lowering rates, it is doing so in a consistent pattern at subsequent meetings until an economic goal is accomplished. Read the FOMC minutes and be sure to keep your ears open for any hint of interest rate change by Chairman Alan Greenspan. He is often quite vocal on the Federal Reserve's objectives for the economy, and you may be able to pick up on the trend of the Federal Reserve adjustments. Generally, if employment levels or GDP growth are too strong, the Federal Reserve is nervous about rising inflation, and you may see a rate increase to stifle the economy. Similarly, if inflation is not threatening and the Federal Reserve feels employment is weak and GDP growth is stagnant, it may lower interest rates to revive the economy.

It is important to note that the Federal Reserve has no direct command over the Federal Funds Rate. You can see from the simplified example that the Federal Reserve only influences the level of interest rates by buying and selling government bonds. What the Federal Reserve does is attempt to influence the Federal Funds Rate to move toward a target average. The target level is determined by the FOMC at each meeting and hence provides a direction for monetary policy. And then the Federal Reserve will buy and sell securities to push the rate to the target level.[4]

But the Federal Reserve does a very good job of keeping the target rate close to the actual rate. Universally, the Federal Reserve receives high marks in this area. "The Fed targets the funds rate, and the overnight federal funds rate stays close, on average, to the Fed's target," write visiting scholar at the Federal Reserve Bank of Atlanta John C. Robertson and assistant vice president and economist at the Federal Reserve Bank of St. Louis Daniel L. Thornton.[5]

To show you how the Federal Funds Rate fluctuates during the day, here is *The Wall Street Journal* federal funds quote (in the Money Rates section) for Friday, August 25, 2000:

Federal funds: $6^{11}/_{16}$% high, $6^3/_8$% low, $6^3/_8$% near closing bid, $6^1/_2$% offered. Reserves traded among commercial banks for overnight use in amounts of \$1 million or more.[6]

You can see how the federal funds rate fluctuates during the day, but the Federal Reserve is successful in keeping the rate close to its target rate. The Federal Reserve monitors the rate continuously and buys bonds and sells bonds daily to keep the rate on target. Essentially, what the Federal Reserve wants is a respectable level of non-inflationary GDP growth.

While Alan Greenspan and his colleagues do not actually get out and buy and sell bonds themselves, they come close. The FOMC issues a directive to the Open Market desk at the New York bank, the operating agent of the Federal Reserve. The trading desk implements the FOMC directive by buying and selling bonds according to the Federal Reserve's wishes. This directive gives general guidelines to the Federal Reserve Bank of New York for the buy or sell orders that will ultimately push up or lower interest rates.

Just how big is trading in the federal funds market? The minimum trading unit is typically $1 million. Because of the size of the market, it is typically the big New York banks trading in federal funds. But even small banks get in on the action. They sell their excess reserves to a big bank that packages up the huge $1 million lots.

Interest rate targets, not monetary targets (although wide growth ranges for M2 and M3 are targeted), are the Federal Reserve's main targets for monetary policy. The Federal Funds Rate is maintained to "foster price stability and promote sustainable growth in output." In plain language, the FOMC wants to maintain strong economic growth coupled with low inflation. Thornton notes, "For some time now, the Federal Reserve has implemented monetary policy by making discrete adjustments to its target for the federal funds rate."[7] Chart 10-1 shows the FOMC's recent adjustments to federal funds. You can see the federal funds target rate increased gradually over this time period, largely initiated by a concern over inflation. Take a peek at Chart 10-2, the monthly tabulation of Federal Funds Rates and you can see how the two are parallel. The Federal Reserve does a great job of buying and selling bonds to keep federal funds close to its target.

Federal funds data is not revised. As you can see, federal funds have been shifting upward during the above-charted period. A major rate drop would give a big boost to bond prices. So keep in mind the basic

Chart 10-1

Federal Reserve
Federal Funds Rate Adjustments

FOMC Meeting	Percent
February 2–3, 1999	4.75%
March 30, 1999	4.75%
May 18, 1999	4.75%
June 29–30, 1999	5.00%
August 24, 1999	5.25%
October 5, 1999	5.25%
November 16, 1999	5.25%
December 21, 1999	5.50%
February 1–2, 2000	5.75%
March 21, 2000	6.00%
May 16, 2000	6.50%
June 27–28, 2000	6.50%
August 22, 2000	6.50%

Source: Minutes and Announcements of
the Federal Open Market Committee

principle: interest rates up and bond prices down, buy; interest rates down and bond prices up, sell.

If You Want to Know More: Types of Bonds

There are many types of bonds you can buy. Investigate and choose options that best satisfy your risk and return objectives. Following are some of the general categories to get you started:

- **Corporate Bonds.** Bonds that are issued by corporations are backed by the company that issues them. The safest bonds are given the highest ratings by the bond rating agencies, like Moody's and Standard & Poor's. Most corporate bonds are debenture bonds, backed only by the company's reputation and ability to repay. Other corporate bonds are secured by select assets of the firm. Generally speaking, the riskier the issue, the higher the return offered. But the majority of corporate bonds are fairly solid issues.

- **Zero-Coupon Bonds.** These bonds, commonly referred to as zeros, pay interest only upon maturity. They sell at huge discounts off the face value and you receive the full principal upon maturity. Zeros are significantly more sensitive to interest rate changes than other bonds. So if rates fall and you sell before maturity, you will likely win big. On the flip side, if rates rise and you must sell before maturity, you may suffer great loss.

- **Government Bonds.** The federal government sells bonds to finance the national debt and ongoing operations. These are the safest bonds to buy because they are backed by the full faith and credit of the federal government. These instruments are often referred to as risk-free securities. But with low risk tends to come low returns. Treasury notes are issued in maturities of one to ten years, with Treasury bonds ranging in longer maturity from ten to thirty years. Interest is free from state and local taxation.

- **International Bonds.** These bonds are issued by foreign governments and businesses. These bonds can pay significantly higher interest rates than their U.S. counterparts. However, you can easily get caught up in the exchange rate dilemma, so look for foreign bonds denominated in U.S. dollars. Foreign bonds can also easily be purchased indirectly through international bond funds.

Chart 10-2

Effective Monthly Federal Funds Rates

May 1999	4.74%
June 1999	4.76%
July 1999	4.99%
August 1999	5.07%
September 1999	5.22%
October 1999	5.20%
November 1999	5.42%
December 1999	5.30%
January 2000	5.45%
February 2000	5.73%
March 2000	5.85%
April 2000	6.02%
May 2000	6.27%
June 2000	6.53%

Source: U.S. Department of Commerce
Bureau of Economic Analysis

☞ **Junk Bonds.** These bonds are a riskier and higher-yielding version of a corporate issue. These bonds will offer a very high interest rate because they have received a low credit rating (or no rating) by the bond rating agencies. One reason may be that the company issuing the debt is new and has not developed a track record of debt repayments yet. Or it could be issued by a company with an already high level of debt and a financially weak position.

☞ **Convertible Bonds**. This is a special type of bond, a hybrid of a bond and stock, that can be converted into a specific number of stock shares of the issuing company. The conversion is at the direction of the bond owner. But the conversion price is always set at a level above the firm's stock price at the time the convertible was issued. While you may never find it advantageous to convert, the plus is that you have a chance to cash in big if the stock of the company does well. As a result of this upside potential, the bond interest rate is less than the typical corporate issue.

☞ **Municipal Bonds.** These bonds are issued by states, cities, towns, and counties, and are predominately revenue bonds and general obligation (GO) bonds. Revenue bonds depend on the revenue generated by the project being financed. For example, toll roads, water systems, utility systems, and airport authorities all charge tolls for their use, and the income will be used to pay the principal and interest on the bond. GOs are backed by the full faith and credit of the issuing municipality. The income from the bond sales of GOs is used to finance general operations of the municipality. Munis, as they are commonly called, have lower interest rates than corporate issues. The main reason is that the interest that they pay is free from federal taxation. And, depending on the state in which you live, you may have exemption from state taxation, as well. Munis tend to be attractive to individuals in high tax brackets, who get a big tax rate break with these bonds.

Business Cycle Activity

As you can see from Chart 10-3, the Federal Funds Rate (monthly index) tends to peak before a recession—around six months prior. You can see the sharp descent in the Federal Funds Rate during the recessionary periods. The Federal Funds Rate is a leading indicator during recessions only. It is a lagging indicator at the economy's troughs, and an expansion is well under way before the rate starts to turn up. The federal funds ride can be particularly bumpy, especially during expansions.

Chart 10-3

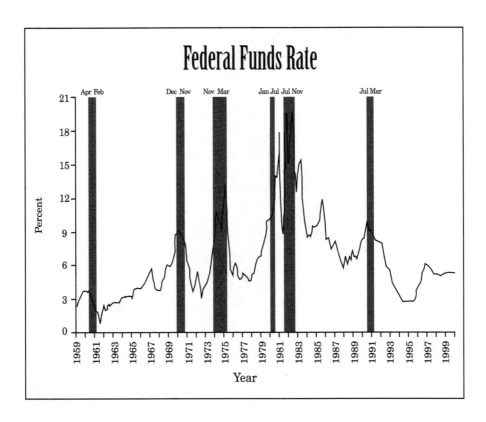

Federal Funds Rate

Source: The Conference Board

Financial Participants' Reaction

If the Federal Reserve raises rates, it is definitely a pity party for the bond market. As interest rates go up, bond prices fall—that is a given. But the stock market is a whole different deal. The market knows that Greenspan and his buddies are inflation fighters. So when inflation rises, even a minor amount, the fear arises that the FOMC will raise rates. The question is "What will the Federal Reserve do with interest rates?" Most of the time the market senses the Federal Reserve's reaction and often even reacts positively to a rate increase if participants feel it will not harm corporate profitability. If, however, a rate increase is larger than anticipated, it can have negative consequences for the market.

Summary

Federal funds are overnight loans between banking institutions. The interest rate paid on these loans is called the Federal Funds Rate. It is the first interest rate indicator to turn down prior to a recession. Not only does it foretell recessions, it efficiently foretells the direction of short-term interest rates. So if you are interested in investing in bonds, be sure to watch and monitor the federal funds rate for hints about the direction of interest rates. You can make money in the bond market by buying bonds when interest rates are high (bond prices are down) and selling bonds when rates are down (when bond prices are back up).

Tracking Federal Funds

Check out the Federal Funds Rate for interest rate clues to profit in the bond market.

Frequency: The indicator is released on a daily basis. To get a feel for small business opportunities, watch the number for at least three quarters and track the trend. If you are planning bond buys and sells, you don't need a big historical track record. You can tell immediately the direction of rates and the effect on bond prices. Check it frequently over the month and plot your move accordingly.

When: The rate changes frequently throughout the day, and the closing bid is generally published.

Where: The Federal Funds Rate is covered on national and local television, and most newspapers. CNNfn gives widespread coverage to this number. It is particularly big news on the day the Federal Reserve meets to consider changing interest rates, which happens about every six weeks. Catch it on a regular basis in such newspapers as the *New York Times,* the *Washington Post,* the *Miami Herald,* the *Tampa Tribune,* the *Los Angeles Times,* the *Chicago Tribune,* the *Oregonian,* the *Houston Chronicle,* and the *San Jose Mercury News* (in Saturday's business section). Many local newspapers also run the number. *USA Today* covers every Federal Reserve meeting and reports the number even when it doesn't change. Additionally, you can always locate the number every day in the Money Rates section of both *The Wall Street Journal* and *Investor's Business Daily.* For consistency, track the last bid rate of the day.

How: The data will be released as a decimal, such as 6.4375. For clues on the direction of the federal funds rate, pay attention to Federal Reserve Chairman Alan Greenspan's interest rate discussions with the press and media.

Use the following chart to track the Federal Funds Rate:

Federal Funds Rate

January	
February	
March	
April	
May	
June	
July	
August	
September	
October	
November	
December	

Notes on Trend:

Chapter 11

Buy Now, Pay Later: The Yield Curve

"What costs nothing is worth nothing."

—Anonymous

For planning your borrowing strategy, you can tell immediately about the structure of rates and your personal debt plan by looking at the difference between the yields on short- and long-term securities. The general pattern of borrowing is to borrow long-term and pay a higher interest rate. Many of us try to pay cash to avoid this situation. But there are occasions when rates are low and it may be worthwhile to take out a long-term loan. There also may be times when long-term rates are so high it will significantly increase your wealth if you can go with a shorter-term loan and hence pay less in interest. Watch the yield curve to know how best to plan your debt strategy. If long-term rates are higher than short-term (or vice versa), this is going to roughly be the spread situation for the entire market interest rate structure.

The yield curve is a graph of interest rates, typically, on Treasury securities. It's not a fancy mathematical model, and just a quick look at the shape of the curve will give you the lowdown on the economy. Most of the time, the yield curve slopes upward. In other words, rates on long-term securities are higher than rates on short-term securities. The reason: investors usually demand a higher interest rate for long-term securities because they must be compensated for the risk involved with tying up funds for a longer period of time. So, for example, you may see a rate of 6.50 percent for a ten-year Treasury security, but a 4.75 percent for a three-month Treasury security. But when short-term rates become higher than long-term rates, the curve slopes downward (or inverts) and a recession generally follows. And the yield curve is one indicator for which you don't need a historical track record. The shape of the curve at any given time will tell you what you need to know.

Are short-term loans ever a good thing? Is it wise to pay off your credit card debt early? If you don't need a loan, should you ever still consider it? What about the upfront cash discounts that are offered? Refinancing—should you make the move? Look to the slope of the yield curve to help you structure your debt.

Where to Find the Yield Curve

There are two ways the daily yield curve can be reported in the media. Either the curve itself is shown and its slope is discussed and analyzed, or the rates for short-term and long-term Treasuries are run, from which the reader or viewer can easily draw a yield curve. National television news programs and many newspapers cover this indicator. CNNfn consistently reports on the yield curve and Treasury rates. Widely available newspapers like the *New York Times,* the *Washington Post,* and *USA Today* publish this indicator. Regional sources providing coverage of this indicator include the *Oregonian,* the *Houston Chronicle,* the *Chicago Tribune,* and Louisville's *Courier-Journal.* And if you miss it on the news, the Treasury yield curve is covered daily in the Credit sections of *The Wall Street Journal* and *Investor's Business Daily.*

For planning your debt strategy, you don't need a long historical track record. You can learn immediately about the structure of rates and be able to plan accordingly by looking at the difference between short- and long-term securities. You'll want to check the yield curve at least a few times a month.

What the Slope Says

You may have heard your stockbroker or a news analyst talk about a yield curve as if it were a magic formula. Not true. It is an easy way to compare the current yields (returns based on the securities' prices) for short-term, mid-term, and long-term securities.

There are three shapes to yield curves (all depicted in Chart 11-1) upward-sloping, downward-sloping, and flat:

- **Upward-sloping.** As you can see, an upward-sloping yield curve is the typical pattern because investors demand a higher interest payment in compensation for loaning their money for longer periods of time. Simply, long-term securities offer higher yields than short-term securities. When long-term rates are a great deal higher than short-term rates, a steeply sloped upward curve emerges. Although not a stellar expansion predictor, a positive interest rate spread suggests the economy may be entering an expansion again.

- **Downward-sloping.** A downward-sloping yield curve emerges when short-term securities have a higher rate than long-term securities, often referred to as an inverted yield curve. This is not the norm and may be a sign that the economy is getting ready to enter a recession.

- **Flat.** In this scenario, the rate on short-term securities has exactly the same rate as securities of a longer maturity. Practically speaking, a perfectly horizontal yield curve would be quite unusual. As short rates begin to rise relative to long-term rates the yield curve begins to flatten out. As the curve begins to flatten, rates may be beginning to invert. Market watchers are particularly tuned in to both downward-sloping and flat yield curves.

Chart 11-1, Types of Yield Curves

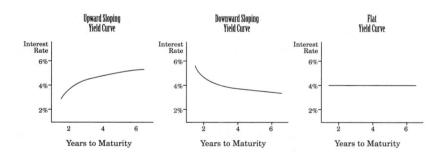

The inversion of the yield curve (downward curve) is an old-time—but still useful—market indicator of tough times ahead. In an article analyzing the predictive value of the yield curve published in the Federal Reserve Bank of Cleveland's Economic Review, authors Joseph G. Haubrich and Ann M. Dombrosky write:

Many market observers carefully track the yield curve's shape, which is typically upward sloping and somewhat convex. At times, however, it becomes flat or slopes downward ["inverts," in Wall Street parlance], configurations that many business economists, financial analysts, and other practitioners regard as harbingers of recession.[1]

An inverted (downward) yield curve, or negative interest spread, has historically signaled a recession. Since 1960, an inverted yield curve has preceded each of the five recessions. "Although the yield curve cannot guarantee good times in the coming year, the track record indicates that no tool offers better clues about the likelihood of coming economic troubles," conclude Federal Reserve Bank of St. Louis economists Dusan Stojanovic and Mark D. Vaughan.[2] The inversion that typically precedes a recession varies greatly, but often begins as much as one to two years ahead of the downturn.

What causes short-term rates to rise above long-term? In the economy, many variables can affect interest rate structure, and there are a number of prevailing economic theories to explain the term structure of interest rates.[3] Likely, the stimulus to move short-term rates over long-term rates comes from two main forces—investor expectations and tight monetary policy.

Business activity rises and interest rates rise, as well, due to high loan demand during expansionary phases. But eventually it happens that, for whatever reason, investors become skittish and expect the boom to slow. When business slows, interest rates tend to fall. Consumers have come to expect declining rates with depressed economic activity. Although savers would be thrilled to lend money long-term and lock into some decent rates before they drop, borrowers simply don't want to tie up funds for long periods of time in a falling interest rate environment. Because borrowers are more interested in short-term securities in this changing environment, the demand for short-term securities will push short-term rates up.

A strict tightening of credit by the Federal Reserve forces short-term rates higher than long-term rates. Conversely, when the Federal Reserve implements an expansionary monetary policy, easing up on money and credit conditions, short-term rates decline compared to long-term rates, with more expansive production following.

Using the Yield Curve

When long-term rates are higher than short-term rates, you will see an upward-sloping yield curve. It's best to go for the shortest loan you can swing. And the steeper the slope, the more advantageous short-term loans are. This means short-term rates are significantly cheaper than long-term. Upfront cash discounts are also probably a good idea when the yield curve is upward-sloping.

It is a widespread practice for professional offices (like doctors, dentists, accounting firms, and law practices), tuition plans, and even utility companies to offer a discount, sometimes as much as 10 percent, if you pay up front for your bill. These opportunities are attractive for consumers, and the businesses win too because they now have more cash liquidity and less chance of default payments. Since you won't be earning much on your short-term investments, take the payment reduction.

When short-term rates are higher than long-term rates you will see a downward-sloping curve. Consider refinancing to capture the lower long-term rates. As soon as you see the curve flatten or invert, run to the bank. Long-term rates have fallen compared to short-term and you may be able to do better on your mortgage or other loans by refinancing. There are two caveats—you must calculate the cost of refinancing (points and fees), if any, against the term of the loan to make sure it would be worth your while, and remember that with a mortgage and some other loans you pay the bulk of the interest at the beginning of the term. If you have paid eight years on a fifteen-year mortgage, or twenty-years on a thirty-year mortgage, it may not make sense to refinance. It also will not make sense even on a newer mortgage if you are not planning to stay in the house long enough to at least recoup your costs of refinancing.

Generally, the most cost efficient strategy would be always to pay outright for your purchases. However, there are circumstances when you can actually use debt as an asset to increase your wealth. Sound too go to be true? It's not, and the situation occurs frequently. When you see a downward slope, short-term rates are universally higher than long-term. Here is your opportunity to repay the loan and make money on the spread. Just for example, if short-term money market rates are 9 percent, and the longer-term personal loan rate is 7 percent, go for the loan. Invest your money in the money market and and make money on the spread. Repay your loan with some of the earnings from the great short-term investment returns. You simply can't pass this one up. Do be sure to calculate any fees associated with the borrowing and make sure the spread is enough to make it worthwhile.

Regardless of the direction of the yield curve, it will almost always be to your advantage to take any extra cash in a short-term account such as a money market, savings account, or checking account, and pay off your credit card debt. Always when there is an upward-sloping curve, it will be to your advantage to pay off your card when long-term rates are really high. But even when you see a slight inversion, it still may be advantageous to pay the card off. The reason is that credit card interest is one of the highest rates you'll pay on debt. And depending on what type of credit card you have, you may carry some elevated rates. So you would need to be earning some very steep interest on your investments to make it worth your while to carry this high interest debt.

Compilation and Release of the Yield Curve

Yield curves may be based on any variety of components. You may see a yield curve based on CD rates, or a curve based on the short-term Federal Funds Rate and a long-term Treasury rate. Regardless of the components, all yield curves tell you the same thing. If it slopes upward, long-term rates are higher than short-term. If it is flat, then short-term rates and long-term rates are roughly equal. And if it slopes downward, short-term rates are higher than long-term rates. Typically, investment companies prepare the published curves. For example, *The Wall Street Journal* receives its yield curves from Banx.com Inc., a New York–based financial information technology company. But if you know a short-term security rate (three-month Treasury, for example) and a long-term rate (ten-year Treasury, for example) you can do the math or simply draw a rough yield curve yourself.

If You Want to Know More: Attributes of Treasury Securities

Since Treasuries are generally used in the Yield Curve, let's investigate the attributes of Treasury securities. This will provide a more complete picture of the purpose and functions Treasuries provide.

When investors buy Treasury securities, they are lending money to the U.S. government. They sell Treasury bills, notes, and bonds to the public to pay off maturing debt and to raise funds needed for the operation of the federal government. The overwhelming majority, 77 percent, of the $5.7 trillion national debt is actually internally held by U.S. businesses, households, and institutions. The remaining 23 percent is held by foreigners. The interest payments on the national debt are certainly nothing to sneeze at, roughly $230 billion per year, but because the majority of the debt is held in the United States, the majority of the interest payments are made to U.S. businesses, households, and institutions.

Treasury obligations are marketable (meaning you can trade the securities with other investors before they mature) and compose close to 60 percent of the national debt.[4] Treasury securities are issued by the Bureau of the Public Debt, which also services and redeems these obligations as part of its mission to finance and account for the public debt. These marketable securities are available through the Internet (www.publicdebt.treas.gov), by phone (800-722-2678), or from a Treasury Direct office. Treasury marketable securities can be resold through financial institutions and government securities brokers and dealers.

Savers view government securities as a great investment because they are a safe way to save money. The federal government always pays back investors. Due to the guarantee of the full faith and credit of the U.S. government, these securities are often referred to as risk-free securities. Because of the safety of Treasuries, the interest rates offered will not be as high as those from similar-term, high-quality corporate bonds. The government offers three types of Treasuries: short-term securities are referred to as Treasury bills, mid-term securities are Treasury notes, and long-term issues are called Treasury bonds.

Treasury Bills: These are short-term securities with a term of one year or less. Treasury bills are high priced—they have a par value of a minimum $10,000. T-bills, as they are commonly called, are sold at a discount from the par (redeemable) value and do not pay interest before maturity. The difference between the purchase price of the bill and the par value is the compensation the investor receives.

Treasury Notes: T-notes are intermediate federal securities with maturities from one to ten years. They bear a stated interest rate that is paid semiannually. The amounts normally range from $1,000 to $5,000, and rates are generally higher than for T-bills.

Treasury Bonds: The longest-term maturity federal obligations are T-bonds, issued with a term of ten to thirty years. These securities are issued in base amounts of $1,000. Just like notes, they pay interest on a semi-annual basis. Interest rates for bonds are typically higher than notes or bills.

Yield Curve Activity

You can see in Chart 11-2 the upward sloping yield curve for Treasuries with maturities up to seven years (in February 2000). Check out Chart 11-3 for a yield curve showing extended Treasuries, all the way to thirty years. A slightly bumpier interest rate ride, but still definitely upward sloping. No recession warning here.

Chart 11-2

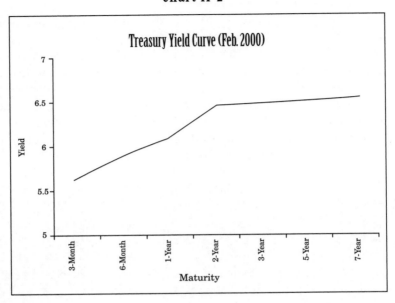

Chart 11-3

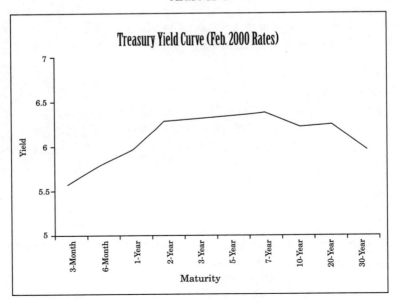

Financial Participants' Reaction

Many financial players watch the yield curve. Market watchers look for narrowing of the spread, which brings concern. As the interest spread starts to invert, market watchers regard it as a possible sign of an upcoming recession.

Summary

An inverted yield curve, or downward slope, has historically preceded a recession. The curve often starts to invert one to two years ahead of an actual recession. Further, a downward slope tells you to get a cheap long-term loan while earning great interest on your short-term investments. Also, consider refinancing to capture lower long-term rates. An upward-sloping curve is the more typical situation, and it tells you that shorter loans are definitely the winners and that upfront cash discounts play in your favor.

Tracking the Yield Curve

Check out the Yield Curve when structuring your debt plan.

Frequency: The indicator is released on a daily basis. To plan your personal debt strategy, you don't need a big historical track record. You can tell immediately about the structure of rates by looking at the difference between short- and long-term securities. Check it at least a few times a month and plan your moves accordingly.

When: There are two ways the yield curve can be reported by the media. Either the curve (or its slope) is shown and discussed and analyzed in a story, or the rates for short-term and long-term Treasuries are run (enabling the reader to draw a yield curve easily).

Where: National television news programs and many newspapers make this indicator available to the public. CNNfn widely reports on the yield curve and Treasury rates. Newspapers such as the *New York Times,* the *Washington Post,* and *USA Today* cover this indicator. Regional publications providing coverage of this indicator include the *Oregonian,* the *Houston Chronicle,* the *Chicago Tribune,* and Louisville's *Courier-Journal.* The Treasury yield curve is also covered daily in the credit section of *The Wall Street Journal* and *Investor's Business Daily.*

How: Check the numbers or the Yield Curve frequently during the month and jot down the direction of the curve. Remember to note the slope of the curve, such as upward sloping, steep upward slope, starting to invert, flattening out, and so on. Look for press and media commentary on the slope of the curve with observations like "starting to invert" or "marked upward slope."

Use the following chart to track the Yield Curve:

Yield Curve

January	
February	
March	
April	
May	
June	
July	
August	
September	
October	
November	
December	

Notes on Trend:

Chapter 12

Inside Information: Leading Economic Indicator

"For also knowledge itself is power."

—Francis Bacon

Short on time? Interested in the economy's performance but don't need the detail the individual indicators provide? The Leading Economic Indicator (LEI) is made for you. If you want one indicator that will give you a clue on broad economic activity, look no further than the LEI. The figure is a compilation of ten numbers that move together ahead of the economy's highs and lows. By simply knowing if the monthly LEI has risen or fallen, you will possess "inside information." Here's the deal. If the LEI has started a notable descent, you can be pretty sure that economic activity will start to take a downward spiral, on average, nine months later. This means that along with depressed real (adjusted for inflation) GDP, virtually all broad economic sectors will be down—unemployment will rise (it is an inverted indicator), the number of big purchases will be low, the housing market will stagnate, the stock market will slump, credit will be tight, business profitability will slow, and interest rates will fall eventually. A steady pick-up of the LEI from a low point means that on average, four months later, the economy will be booming and will enter an expansion. Along with an increasing real GDP figure, unemployment will be falling, the number of big purchases will climb, the housing market will take off, the stock market will skyrocket, credit will be widely available, business profitability will boom, and interest rates will ultimately rise.

It couldn't be easier. Just check out this widely published monthly figure and you will have the inside economic scoop on the economy's movement. Read on to discover more about the LEI and how it can help you.

Where to Find the LEI

The monthly LEI is published with an approximate five-week lag from the data month. When announced, it is released early in the morning and receives prominent coverage on that day and the day following on national television news programs. CNNfn routinely reports on this monthly number. Coverage in newspapers generally takes place the day after the statistic is reported on television. Check out the LEI in big papers like the *New York Times* and the *Washington Post. USA Today* doesn't cover it on a regular basis, but often will include it as part of a larger story. Regional publications that often report on the number include the *Oregonian,* the *Chicago Tribune,* Louisville's *Courier-Journal,* the *Miami Herald,* and the *Houston Chronicle.* The story will be released in other regional newspapers only if it is an unusually strong or weak number.

On a regular schedule, you can find the LEI in *The Wall Street Journal* (in the Economy section) and *Investor's Business Daily* (in the Business & Economy section), appearing the day after its release. Also, you can call (212) 339-0330 for a recorded message listing LEI data for the last three months.

To get a general feel for the direction of upcoming economic activity, check out the monthly LEI for at least three months.

What the Number Says

Regardless of the reporting source, you will generally see at least two numbers connected to the LEI each month. You will see the amount of the drop or fall from the previous month and the resulting total for the index. You could see, for example, that the index rose .2 percent last month to 108.4. An increase in the index hints that the economy will start to grow shortly. As a predictor of business cycles, a bottoming out in the index with subsequent rises suggests the economy will enter an expansion shortly. Or you may see the opposite. For example, the index fell .1 percent last month to 108.1. A drop in the index suggests that the economy will slow in the coming months. As an indication of a new phase of the business cycle, a peak in the LEI and subsequent falling numbers suggests the economy will be entering a recession shortly.

The LEI numbers are simple to read. Negative contributions are seen as bad news for the economy. Positive contributions are seen as favorable for the economy's growth. While the index is not foolproof, it does have a staunch record of reliability. The compilation of ten leading indicators together has strong predictive ability. Couple the number with your observations of the economy, some good old common sense, and you will have a good idea of what is likely to happen in the future. Let's investigate how the LEI can be so helpful with all your daily money decisions.

Using the LEI

The LEI essentially provides us with a complete overview of economic performance. Chart 12-1 provides a checklist of major economic sectors and their likely activity shortly after the LEI rises or falls. When the LEI is rising, it suggests that very soon these broad major sectors will be moving up as well, with the exception of interest rates, which lag the economy. Expect an expansion soon if the index has bottomed out and is moving upward. Interest rates generally turn up after the economy has already entered an expansion and some time after the LEI has bottomed out and started to move up.

When the LEI falls we can anticipate that in the coming months these major sectors will be moving down. Interest rates will likely move down too (excluding federal funds which is a leader at recessions), but with more of a lag. Rates generally turn down after the economy has entered a recession and long after the LEI has turned down. Once the LEI has started to turn down, you can at least count on a slowdown in the major sectors. If the LEI has peaked and started downward, suspect a recession coming in a matter of months.

Chart 12-1

LEI Shifts
Likely future sector activity

	When LEI is rising:	When LEI is falling:
Unemployment	Falling	Rising
Big Purchases	Rising	Falling
Housing	Rising	Falling
Stock Market	Rising	Falling
Credit	Rising	Falling
Business Profitability	Rising	Falling
Interest Rates	Rising with lag	Falling with lag

Here is a simplified scenario of how the economic variables work together. Four months before the expansion begins, the LEI turns up, and starts showing positive numbers. One of the main ingredients that propels us out of a recession and into an expansion is increased spending—predominately by consumers and businesses. Because the government has an ever-ready source of funds from borrowing and taxing, it has more of a tendency for level spending (unless it is war spending). Shortly, consumers will be spending more on virtually everything— more on housing, durable goods purchases, and nondurable purchases (like personal care items and personal services). Business firms will be spending more on big capital orders and expansion plans. They will be developing new products, expanding facilities, adding stores, and hiring more employees. Business sales and profitability will skyrocket from the increased spending. Expect credit to be widely available during the boom. Businesses will compete for money to finance new expansion projects, consumers will be more inclined to take on more debt when times appear good, and eventually rates will start to surge upward. This competing will put upward pressure on rates. And when the boom is on, consumers catch the craze and invest heavily in the stock market.

But all good things must come to an end. On the flip side, an average of just under nine months before a recession hits, the LEI turns down and starts showing negative numbers. Soon all business activity will be depressed. When business spending falls, firms cut back on expansion plans, inventories pile up, and employees are let go. Once a decrease in spending takes place, it significantly alters the chance for an economic recovery. The die has been cast. Expect consumers to cut back on their spending, particularly in large purchases like housing and durable items, both of which are expensive and are generally postponed to better times. The lack of consumer and business spending will hit the business bottom line hard. And because businesses are not expanding, and consumers become uneasy about taking on more debt, there is a lack of loan demand. This lack of loan demand allows interest rates to come back down. But again, look for a delayed reaction. Most rates actually peak after the economy has just entered a recession, and then start to slide. When the recession hits, the entire stock market, organized and over-the-counter exchanges, will be in a slump too.

So how can you use the information to your advantage? Here are just a few things to keep in mind:

- **Unemployment:** If the LEI is rising, the entire national unemployment picture will be better shortly (a hint that it will be a great time for job hunting). If the LEI is falling, soon the entire national unemployment picture will worsen (a hint not to make any risky job moves until times are better).

- **Big Purchases:** If the LEI is rising, both consumers and firms will increase big-ticket item purchases in the near future (a clue that the stores will be full soon, and sales will be plentiful). If the LEI is falling, both consumers and firms will be quick to decrease big-ticket item purchases (a clue that store selection and competitive pricing won't be there).

- **Housing:** If the LEI is rising, the entire housing market—new homes and existing homes—will boom shortly (a red flag that housing demand will be strong and it will be a great time to sell). If the LEI is falling, soon the entire housing market—new homes and existing homes—will go bust (a red flag that some recession housing steals are sure to become available).

- **Stock Market:** If the LEI is rising, expect that all the stock exchanges and stock prices will skyrocket (a cue to watch your stock prices—you may be able to sell high). If the LEI is falling, all the stock exchanges and stock prices will fall in the near future (a cue that some great buys may be on the horizon).

- **Credit:** If the LEI is rising, the economy will become more liquid and credit will be widely available (a hint that it will be an easy time to get a loan). If the LEI is falling, the economy will become less liquid soon, and credit will be constrained (an indication that the loan opportunities are going to become more competitive).

- **Business Profitability:** If the LEI is rising, expect big business and small business profitability to rise (a suggestion that, if you are considering opening or buying an enterprise, it is a profitable time to enter the business world). If the LEI is falling, watch for big business and small business profitability to slack off (a warning to exercise caution in any new business venture).

- **Interest Rates:** If the LEI is rising, interest rates likely will rise, although with a considerable lag (an indication that you should lock in a loan rate before they skyrocket, or hold out for the coming higher investment rates). If the LEI is falling, interest rates likely will fall, although with a considerable lag (an indication that you

should wait for the coming low loan rates, or grab the great investment rates before they fall).

Compilation and Release of the Number

If you are interested in precision concerning an individual economic
component, the LEI is not your thing. Look to the specific individual leading indicators for hints of highs and lows in their representative sectors.
You can look to the ten components that make up the LEI. Components
individually covered in this book are unemployment insurance claims,
building permits, S&P 500, M2 money supply, and the interest rate
spread. Additional components include the average length of the manufacturing work week, manufacturers' new orders for consumer goods and
materials, the speed of supplier deliveries, the index of consumer expectations, and manufacturers' new orders for non-defense capital goods.
The press and media often report directional changes of the components
with the LEI report. Interestingly, most of these numbers have very solid
individual economic forecasting power as well. The individual indicators
have a general tendency to move together. And although each is
respectable in its own right, no single indicator performs quite as well as
the LEI. The advantage of the LEI is that it tends to smooth out a great
deal of the volatility of the ten components to give you a clearer picture
of the economy's overall movement.

The LEI has been publicly reported since 1968. Through the years,
components of the LEI have been dropped while others have been
added, to arrive at the figure that most accurately leads the economy's
performance. The Conference Board last revised the leading index in
December 1996.[1] At that time, the index went from eleven component
figures to the current ten. Because changes in sensitive materials prices
and changes in unfilled orders for durable goods tended to give false
alarms for recessions and expansions, they were both dropped. The
interest rate spread—ten-year Treasury bonds less federal funds—was
added to total ten components. In addition, minor changes were made to
the methods used to calculate other component series.

The LEI has undergone and met numerous statistical and economic
tests. The figure has largely satisfied the following testing requirements:

1. Conformity to the general business cycle;
2. Consistent timing as a leading indicator, with economic significance
   based on generally accepted business cycle theories;
3. Statistical adequacy by way of a reliable data collection process;
4. Smoothness in month-to-month movements; and
5. Currency through a reasonably prompt publication schedule.[2]

Rest assured, the indicators included in the LEI have undergone significant testing to be included in the index. And although the LEI has occasionally missed turning points and generated some false alarms, researchers are constantly studying the LEI's forecasting ability and have attempted to improve its performance through the latest revision. Feel confident that the LEI can forecast future economic activity. Although the cyclical record of foretelling peaks and troughs is fairly respectable, always remember to use your intuition by observing your economic environment. Sometimes your instinct is better than all the numbers in the world.

It has long been reported that a three-month decline in the LEI signals a recession. Old-time LEI watchers viewing three months of decline, such as −.3 percent, −.4 percent and −.5 percent, may automatically forecast a recession. This rule is certainly not tried and true. A lot of research suggests that this rule should be used with great caution. It has trouble discriminating between a true recession and a dampening of economic growth. The professional community often dismisses the rule as being too one-dimensional to be legitimate.[3] The rule has provided at least one false signal during six of the past eight expansions. It tends to overreact to short-run shifts in the LEI.[4] Before a recession forewarning can even be considered, a more dependable indication is a decline during a six-month time frame of between 1 to 2 percent for the leading index, coupled with declines in the majority of the individual components.[5]

To see how LEI movements are interpreted for the economy's future economic performance, following is a story from *The Wall Street Journal* covering the March 1999 data month that showed the LEI was on a roll:

> The index of leading economic indicators rose 1% to 107.3 in March, the sixth monthly increase in a row.
>
> The Conference Board, a private New York research firm, said the March increase follows a revised 0.3% increase in February. The leading indicator index is designed to predict economic activity six to nine months down the road. The February increase was revised up from 0.2% to 107.2.
>
> "Because the leading index is up 1.6% since September of last year, there is a lot of confidence that this expansion will continue at a robust pace," said Michael Boldin, The Conference Board's director of business-cycle research.[6]

The LEI is useful for signaling a directional change in economic activity. So watch mainly for directional changes in the LEI. If declines exist for a number of months in a row, at the very least you have cause for concern. A negative in the LEI for several consecutive months alerts suspicion that a recession may be on the horizon. A number of months of positive changes in the LEI suggests expansion or a continued upsurge. Don't analyze the magnitude of the changes in the LEI; leave this for the professional economists. You should be looking for directional changes only. Again, increases are a sign of prosperous times for the economy. Decreases are a bad sign, suggesting the economy will slow in the coming months.

If You Want to Know More: The Conference Board

Historically, the publication of the LEI resided with the BEA. However, in May 1995, after reevaluating its existing programs and priorities and acknowledging its limited resources, the BEA announced that it intended to terminate its business cycles indicators program. This decision involved turning over not only the LEI but the BEA's coincident and lagging indicators as well. After soliciting proposals from a number of private organizations, The Conference Board was chosen to track these indicators. After a brief transition period, in December 1995, full responsibility for the business cycle indicators program was assumed by The Conference Board. The transition has gone smoothly. The Conference Board compiles and releases the LEI and the other composite numbers in a timely manner. In its efforts to improve reliability of the numbers, The Conference Board also promotes considerable research in the area of business cycle indicators.

The Conference Board, founded in 1916, is a not-for-profit, non-advocacy organization. Although located in New York, The Conference Board has members from more than three thousand organizations in sixty-seven countries. This worldwide research and business membership group is one of the premier private sources of economic and business knowledge. It produces a number of business reports and periodicals, holds conferences and seminars, and conducts peer group councils for senior business executives. The mission of the organization is to improve the business enterprise system and enhance the contribution of business to society.

The LEI is not a volatile index, and any revisions are very small. The Conference Board provides an initial value for the data month plus possible revisions for the past six months. Revisions covering changes outside the six-month period are made each December. Usually, any revisions are so small they are not even reported by the popular press, so for tracking purposes, don't be concerned with updates.

Chart 12-2

The Leading Index

Leading index component data	November 1999	December 1999
Average workweek: production workers, mfg. (hours)	41.7	41.7p
Average weekly initial claims: state unemployment insurance (thousands)*	286.5	285.1
Manufacturer's new orders: consumer goods and materials (in millions, 1992 dollars)	169,014r	171,857p
Vendor performance: slower deliveries, diffusion index (percent)	56.1r	56.7
Manufacturer's new orders: nondefense capital goods (in millions, 1992 dollars)	50.813r	55,225p
Building permits (thousands)	1,612	1,622
Stock prices: 500 common stocks © (index: 1941-43=100)	1,391.00	1,428.68
Money supply: M2 (in billions, 1992 dollars)	4,025.3r	4,049.4p
Interest rate spread: 10-year Treasury bonds less federal funds	.61	.98
Index of consumer expectations © (1966:1=100)	101.0	101.1

Leading index net contributions	November 1999	December 1999
Leading Index (1992=100)	108.3	108.7
Percent change from preceding month	.3	.4p
Average workweek: production workers, mfg.	-.03	.00p
Average weekly initial claims: state unemployment insurance	.01	.01
Manufacturers' new orders: consumer goods and materials	.10r	.05p
Vendor performance: slower deliveries, diffusion index	-.01r	.02
Manufacturers' new orders: nondefense capital goods	-.03	.07p
Building permits	.01	.01
Stock prices: 500 common stocks ©	.13	.05
Money supply: M2	.07r	.11p
Interest rate spread: 10-year Treasury bonds less federal funds	-.06	.08
Index of consumer expectations ©	.04	.00

Key   p = Preliminary   r = Revised   n.a. = Not Available   c = Corrected

*Inverted series—a negative change in this componenet makes a positive contribution.

© = Copyrighted. Stock prices: Standard & Poor's Corporation; Index of consumer expectations, University of Michigan's Survey Research Center.

Calculation Note: The percent change in the index does not always equal the sum of the net contributions of the individual components because of rounding effects and base-value differences.

Source: The Conference Board

The LEI has a stellar track record at predicting recessions. It has
foretold each of the last eight recessions since 1950.

Calculating the Figure

Okay, I'll admit it: I'm glad we don't have to calculate the LEI. It is a
big number-crunching event. As what might be considered a data luxury,
the final monthly LEI is publicly available. In viewing Chart 12-2 you
can see the data for each of the ten components and following, the contributions each makes to the total LEI figure. The Conference Board website and, generally, *The Wall Street Journal* are among the sources that
provide such detail.

Viewing the monthly press release information gives you an idea how
The Conference Board interprets the movement in the LEI and its component shifts. The Conference Board's press release for the composite
indicators for December 1999 noted:

> The leading index increased 0.4 percent…The leading indicators point
> to a continuation of the expansion during 2000.[7]

You can see how virtually all of the indicators, nine out of ten, rose
from November to December. The only one that did not change was
the average workweek. That is okay. On occasion, you will see one or
more figures stay constant or move in a different direction than the
others. It is why we like to view a composite index. We go with the
influence of the majority, so to speak. The average workweek was 41.7
hours for both November and December. But all the other indicators
went up, showing that the economy's performance is still rising and
going stronger. For example, the largest contributor to the LEI was
money supply. Mathematically, this contributed .11 of the .40 percent
change from the previous month. Money supply went from $4,025.3
billion in November to $4,049.4 billion in December. To summarize:
money supply rose, we then spent more, and this increased economic
performance. So the increased money supply made a positive contribution to the LEI. The other eight indicators made positive contributions to the escalating LEI total number, suggesting upcoming
expanding business activity.

This is common. During an expansionary phase, the LEI will rise.
November 1999 was 108.3, and the December 1999 total was 108.7. But
what we really key in on is the jump from one month to the next, .40

percent in this case. A string of positive readings would signal prosperity. A string of declines would signal depressed economic growth.

Accuracy of the Index

The LEI, like all the other indicators in this book, provides rough approximations of economic activity that is likely to occur in the future. Even the chief of the BEA's former Business Cycle Indicators branch, Barry A. Beckman, recommended prudence in an article summarizing the BEA's experience with the business cycle indicators program. He noted, "As a forecasting tool, the leading index must be used with caution and supplemented with other data and information."[8] So Beckman's words reinforce the lesson to monitor the LEI, observe the economy around you, read about the economy's performance, and then ultimately go with your good judgment.

Chart 12-3

Timing of the LEI at Cyclical Turning Points

Leads (-) or lags (+) at business cycle peaks (months)

April 1960	-11
December 1969	-8
November 1973	-9
January 1980	-15
July 1981	-3
July 1990	-6*

Leads (-) or lags (+) at business cycle troughs (months)

February 1961	-3
November 1970	-7
March 1975	-1
July 1980	-3
November 1982	-8
March 1991	-2

*-25 for absolute peak in cycle
Source: Business Cycle Indicators

As you can see in Chart 12-3, the LEI leads recessions, on average, just under nine months (8.67 months). The LEI leads expansions under a shorter time table, an average of four months. That means, on average, around nine months before a recession hits, the LEI starts turning down (begins to show negative contributions). On average, four months before an expansion period begins, the LEI turns up (begins showing positive contributions). Pointing to the unique diversity of each noted business cycle, the LEI pinpoints recessions anywhere from three months all the way to fifteen months prior to a downturn. The noted expansions are foretold anywhere from one to eight months.

Chart 12-4

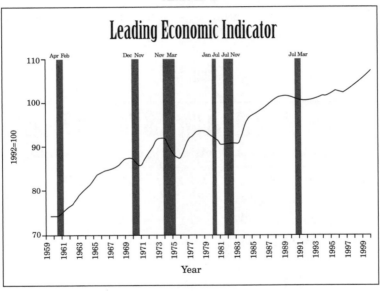

Business Cycle Activity

As you can see from Chart 12-4, the LEI starts to turn down a few months prior to a recession. It falls during a recession. Then the LEI starts to pick up a few months before economic activity begins expanding again and rises during the expansion.

Financial Participants' Reaction

Although the LEI is a vital report for interpreting upcoming economic activity, it is not a big market-mover. There are two likely reasons for the lack of reaction: 1) the individual component data have largely already been released, many of which caused the stock and bond markets to react, and 2) because component numbers are available, the statistical calculation of the LEI generally does not elicit major surprises.

When surprises do occur, bond players react positively to weak LEI numbers. The reason? Weak LEI figures suggest weak growth. Depressed economic growth suggests dampening interest rate pressures. And when interest rates fall, bond prices will rise. So bond players like declines in the LEI.

If a calculation surprise occurs, the reaction from the stock market depends on the current state of concern over the economy. If overwhelming interest rate concerns are not prevailing, the market will rise on word of a surprisingly large increase in the LEI.

Summary

The LEI, one simple number, provides a sign of where the economy will be roughly four to nine months from now, pinpointing recessions and expansions in advance. Understanding the LEI can give a strong hint about unemployment, big-ticket purchases, housing, the stock market, credit availability, business profitability, and interest rates. Watch the nightly news, check out a financial publication, listen to the radio, and log on to the Internet. The LEI report will be there. And although not perfect, the LEI is a huge statistical clue about economic performance. How's that for being on the inside?

Tracking the Leading Economic Indicator

Check out the widely published LEI to get a ballpark idea on how the economy is operating.

Frequency: The indicator is released on a monthly basis. To get a general feel for the direction of upcoming economic activity, check out the LEI for at least three months.

When: The monthly LEI is published with an approximate five-week lag from the data month. When announced, it is released early in the morning.

Where: The number receives prominent coverage in national television news on the day of its release and the day following. CNNfn routinely reports on this monthly number. Coverage in newspapers is generally found the following day. Check out the LEI in national papers such as the

New York Times and the *Washington Post. USA Today* coverage is not on a regular basis but often appears as part of a larger story. Regional publications routinely reporting on the number include the *Oregonian,* the *Chicago Tribune,* the *Houston Chronicle,* the *Miami Herald,* and Louisville's *Courier-Journal.* The story appears in other regional newspapers if it is an unusually strong or weak number. You can find the LEI reported regularly in *The Wall Street Journal* (in the Economy section) and *Investor's Business Daily* (in the Business & Economy section) on the day after its release. Also, you can call (212) 339-0330 for a recorded message listing LEI data for the last three months.

How: The press and television news generally will report the total number for the LEI (such as 105.7) along with a percentage change for the respective month (such as a 0.2 percent decrease for October). Positive changes suggest upcoming strength in the economy, and negative changes indicate a slowdown.

Use the following chart to track the Leading Economic Indicator:

Leading Economic Indicator

January	
February	
March	
April	
May	
June	
July	
August	
September	
October	
November	
December	

Notes on Trend:

Chapter 13

Make Smart Money Decisions

"Wealth is known to be a great comforter."

—Plato

Economic indicators lead, coincide with, or lag economic activity. Although all three types of indicators are valuable for economists monitoring the economy's progress, this book has analyzed nine leading indicators. We simply want to be ahead of the game, to take a sneak peek into the economy's ups and downs. Because these indicators are leading, you get months of advance time to plan your money decisions. You can start to plan your money moves long before the economy enters a recession or expansion. You will have plenty of time to line up the most advantageous job moves, organize big purchases like appliances, cars, and computers, invest wisely in strong stocks, look for a deal in the housing market, plan for a loan, start up or buy an existing business, make money in the bond market, and go for the best credit terms. These are all steps that impact your pocketbook in a big way.

Tracking Is Simple

After reading this book, you can now watch the nightly news, listen to the radio, or read the newspaper with a new degree of economic intelligence. Simply watching, listening to, or reading the business news will allow you to make an educated approximation of upcoming economic activity. Of course, it is advantageous to keep track and chart the indicators so you can more easily see trends emerging. It is easy to track the numbers. You can follow the indicators using index cards or in your date-book or a notebook. For charting specific indicators, you may prefer to use the tracking sheets provided at the end of each chapter. Or for a great overview of all the indicators, use the tracking chart provided at the end of this chapter, useful for tracking the nine indicators plus the real GDP benchmark. For a complete feel of upcoming economic performance, group charting is advantageous. With a data sheet of all the indicators, you will more quickly see broad trends up or down emerging in the economy. Each year, copy a new tracking chart and you will be on your way.

Tips

Keep in mind that economic indicators are a tool, the object of which is to provide information about the trend of economic activity and thereby to enhance your resulting money decisions. Economic indicators are not foolproof. Situations occur where indicators do turn down, but the economy does not; or indicators turn up and the economy does not follow. Leading indicators can turn late. And historical relationships with the economy do change over time. What is a good leading indicator today may not necessarily be a good leading indicator twenty years from now. So you must always use your common sense when evaluating the numbers. Your sound judgment combined with the economic data will result in an on-the-money forecast.

Don't be afraid to consult with experts in your area. Many communities have economic clubs—great sources of economic information—and universities and colleges commonly sponsor economic development seminars. Tune into the local business forecast with new zeal. Many report on local economic indicators, such as area unemployment, inflation, and output. Some even have local stock indicators based on area stocks. These local indicators are generally produced by the local university or college economics department or Chamber of Commerce. When you find these, you have located a real gold mine of knowledge for your local economy. You may even want to track local indicators.

Go Forth

Everyone has easy access to economic data. We live in an information society. Cable television, radio, the Internet, and newspapers provide instantaneous hoards of data. The trick is not in simply hearing or seeing the numbers; anyone can do that. The trick is knowing what the key indicators are, what they mean, and what a change in the numbers means. Many people recognize economic terms but know little, if anything, about them. You now are among a select group that understands nine very significant economic indicators that lead the economy. Use that information wisely to better plan your personal money decisions. Half of the battle is not being intimidated by the jargon and data that surround the reports.

Watch for Other Indicators

To be useful, an indicator is only as good as its track record. The nine indicators cited in this book possess a solid historical record as leading economic activity. Monitor these nine and keep your eye open for emerging trends. Economic indicators are the key to forecasting economic activity and planning your important money moves, so you never want to miss a good leading indicator. Some economists believe that the size of Alan Greenspan's briefcase on his way into Federal Reserve meetings has been a leading indicator of the direction of interest rates. As the theory goes, if his briefcase is thick, it contains documentation for an adjustment in interest rates. Thin briefcase? Relax, rates are staying put. (Just because it's simple doesn't mean it doesn't work!)

Once you have made the nine economic indicators in this book your friends, allies, and tools, you may discover other local or national indicators that become your own personal favorites. Whether you're tracking all nine from this book, some of the nine, or your own personal indicators, watching the economy will surely enhance your finances.

Use this chart to keep track of the indicators you are watching.

Indicator Tracking Chart

Indicator	Real GDP			
	Q1 Jan. Feb. Mar.	Q2 Apr. May Jun.	Q3 Jul. Aug. Sep.	Q4 Oct. Nov. Dec.
Unemployment (released every Thursday)				
Durable Goods Order (released approximately three weeks after the end of the data month)				
Building Permits (released on the twelfth working day of the month after the end of the data month)				
S&P 500 (released daily)				
M2 Money Supply (monthly figure released every Thursday)				
Federal Funds Rate (released daily)				
The Yield Curve (released daily; identify upward or downward slope)				
Leading Economic Indicator (released approximately five weeks from the end of the data month)				
Corporate Profits After Tax (released late in the second month after the close of the quarter)				
Total				

Durable goods orders, building permits, M2 money supply, and the Leading Economic Indicator are released in monthly totals. For the weekly Unemployment Insurance Claims and the daily S&P 500, Federal Funds Rate, and Yield Curve, jot down an average monthly figure. Corporate Profits After Tax is a quarterly figure. Indicators are usually published the day following their release in *The Wall Street Journal* and *Investor's Business Daily*. You can also catch most of the numbers in the *New York Times,* the *Washington Post,* and *USA Today,* as well as from many regional newspapers. Coverage of the indicators on national business news programs, including CNNfn, generally runs the day of the release and the day following. Consult the specific chapter for each indicator to obtain detailed coverage information.

Appendix

Notes to the Reader

The indicator charts in the text, which plotted the indicator data during recessions and expansions, were prepared using data from the Conference Board's Business Cycle Indicators (BCI) database. The BCI database provides economic indicators that have proven to be most useful in determining current conditions and predicting the future direction of the economy. The BCI dataset offers the convenience of a wealth of more than 250 economic/statistical series gathered together in a common format. For further information on BCI, subscription is available for a fee from the Conference Board's Internet site: www.tcb-indicators.org.

For the indicators featured in this book tabulated in convenient monthly form (you will need to graph the Yield Curve from the short-term and long-term U.S. Treasury rates), along with quarterly Corporate Profits After Tax, check out Business Cycle Indicators. For $120 per year, this monthly publication contains both graphs and tables that cover more than 250 series, along with related economic research summaries. Call (212) 339-0345 to subscribe.

Numerous excellent Internet sources providing economic indicators not mentioned in the text are available. Here are just a few favorites that are available free of charge:

The White House's Economic Statistics Briefing Room (www.whitehouse.gov). Click on the White House's home page and go to the Briefing Room, federal statistics. The Economic Statistics Briefing Room provides access to the majority of government indicators featured in this book and a host of other federal economic indicators. All data is updated by the statistical unit of the producing agency and is the most current available. The categories and extensive components include: Employment, Income, International, Money, Output, Prices, Production, and Transportation.

The Council of Economic Advisers' Economic Report to the President (w3.access.gpo/eop/index.html). If you want to quickly find historical figures for government economic indicators, consult the *Economic Report to the President*. All government statistics featured in this book appear in some variation or format, along with many others. Statistical tables are available from the following categories: National Income or Expenditure; Population, Employment, Wages, and Productivity; Production and Business Activity; Prices; Money Stock, Credit, and Finance; Government Finance; Corporate Profits and Finance; Agriculture; and International Statistics. How far back does the data go? The majority begins in the 1950s, but a few go back as far as 1929.

The Dismal Scientist (www.dismal.com). Current and comprehensive, this website can't be beat and is a favorite of economists. You can spend hours browsing here and reading the fantastic current features articles. Click on "United States Economic Releases" and prepare to be impressed by the breadth of the data (many of the indicators featured in this book are covered), summaries, and analyses of the indicators.

Notes

Notes: Chapter 3

1 "Gross Domestic Product as a Measure of U.S. Production," Survey of Current Business, U.S. Department of Commerce Bureau of Economic Analysis, August 1991, p. 8.

2 Bruce T. Grimm and Robert T. Parker, "Reliability of the Quarterly and Annual Estimates of GDP and Gross Domestic Income," Survey of Current Business, U.S. Department of Commerce Bureau of Economic Analysis, December 1998, p. 12.

3 For a detailed summary description of the sources and methods used to prepare the GDP estimates, see "Updated Summary NIPA Methodologies," Survey of Current Business, U.S. Department of Commerce Bureau of Economic Analysis, September 1998, pp. 14–35.

4 Grimm and Parker, p. 13.

5 The IRS currently permits up to $1,200 a year, in cash, to be paid to a domestic worker in your home. After that level it must be reported, and Social Security and Medicare taxes must be paid. For further details consult, "Household Employer's Tax Guide, Publication 926," Department of the Treasury, Internal Revenue Service, Rev. November 1999.

6 This is a peak-to-peak measurement of business cycles. Business cycles can be measured alternatively from trough to trough, which will result in a different duration for the business cycle.

7 "Business Cycle Chronology," NBER Reporter (Cambridge: National Bureau of Economic Research, Fall 1999), p. 3.

Notes: Chapter 4

1 Don't confuse initial claims (released by the Employment and Training Administration of the U.S. Department of Labor) with the monthly unemployment rate (released by the Bureau of Labor Statistics of the U.S. Department of Labor). The unemployment rate has a short lead time for recessions and lags at recoveries.

2 For an excellent detailed description of moving averages and seasonality see *The Economist Numbers Guide: The Essentials of Business Numeracy* (New York: John Wiley & Sons, Inc., 1997), pp. 98–106.

3 Yochi J. Dreazen, "Labor Costs Continued to Climb in June," *The Wall Street Journal,* July 28, 2000, A2.

4 At top, the expansion between December 1982 and June 1990 experienced two strings of four consecutive rises in the weekly adjusted claims data.

5 At top, the July 1990–March 1991 recession experienced two strings of two consecutive falls in the weekly adjusted claims numbers.

6 "ETA Mission Statement," U.S. Department of Labor Employment and Training Administration (www.doleta.gov/mission.htm), February 13, 2000, p. 1.

7 "Unemployment Insurance Claims," U.S. Department of Labor Employment and Training Administration (www.doleta.gov/programs/claims.htm), February 13, 2000, p. 1.

8 "Fact Sheet-Unemployment Insurance," U.S. Department of Labor Employment and Training Administration (www.wdsc.org/layoff/ui.htm), February 13, 2000, p. 1.

9 Steve Slavin, *Economics: A Self-Teaching Guide,* 2nd ed. (New York: John Wiley & Sons, Inc., 1999), p. 117.

10 Ibid., p. 118.

Notes: Chapter 5

1 For a listing of the detailed subcomponents of the industry groupings, see "Manufacturers' Shipments, Inventories, and Orders (M3): Technical Documentation U.S. Department of Commerce," U.S. Department of Commerce Bureau of the Census, 1998.

2 The expansionary consumer durable purchase buying strategy is in sharp contrast to buying a home. Your home, discussed in chapter 6, is the single largest purchase you will make in your lifetime. Because of low mortgage costs, coupled with better prices available from builder and homeowner overextensions, a recessionary home buying strategy is recommended.

3 "Manufacturers' Shipments, Inventories, and Orders (M3) Survey," U.S. Department of Commerce Bureau of Census (www.census.gov/indicator/www/m3/m3desc.htm), February 26, 2000, p. 6.

4 For a description of the seasonal adjustment to new orders, see "Manufacturers' Shipments, Inventories, and Orders (M3) Survey," p. 3.

5 "Advance Report on Durable Goods Manufactures' Shipments and Orders (June 2000)," Press Release, U.S. Department of Commerce Bureau of the Census, July 27, 2000.

6 Hilary Stout, "Durable-Goods Orders Fell 3.2% in June after 4.2% Gain," *The Wall Street Journal,* July 26, 1990, A2.

7 Following are the detailed subcomponents included in transportation equipment:

- Motor vehicles and parts
- Complete aircraft, missiles, and space vehicles, except for the Department of Defense
- Complete aircraft, missiles, and space vehicles for the Department of Defense
- Aircraft, missile, and space vehicle engine and parts, except for the Department of Defense
- Aircraft, missile, and space vehicle engine and parts for the Department of Defense
- Aircraft, missile, and space vehicle engine and parts
- Ships and tank components, except for the Department of Defense
- Ships, tanks, and tank components for the Department of Defense
- Ships, tanks, and tank components
- Railroad equipment
- Other transportation equipment

8 Another data number to view is durable goods, excluding defense. Defense orders tend to exhibit some volatility.

Notes: Chapter 6

1 If your news source routinely publishes housing starts in lieu of permits, it certainly is acceptable to track this number. Both permits and starts provide insight into housing and the general direction of economic performance. Housing starts closely follow permits and are an excellent alternative for tracking. Plan on tracking starts over a five-month period, as opposed to three months for permits.

2 For an excellent analysis of interest rates and their relation to economic activity, see Ronald W. Melicher, Merle T. Welshans, and Edgar A. Norton, Finance: Introduction to Institutions, Investments & Management, 9th ed. (Cincinnati: South-Western Publishing Co., 1997), p. 224.

3 "Housing Starts and Building Permits in January 2000," Press Release, U.S. Department of Commerce Bureau of the Census, February 16, 2000.

4 For an explanation of the seasonally adjusted estimates of building permits, see "Housing Units Authorized by Building Permits," U.S. Department of Commerce Bureau of Census (www.census.gov/const/www/C40/c40text.html), March 1, 2000, p. 5.

5 Jonathan Nicholson, "U.S. Housing Starts +1.5% to 1.775 Million

Rate in January," Dow Jones News Service, February 16, 2000.

6 These numbers, as calculated by The Conference Board, are preliminary because they have not undergone a final review. They are based upon business cycle turning points from 1948 to 1999.

Notes: Chapter 7

1 Just to give you an idea of the multitude of stock market indexes, *The Wall Street Journal* lists twenty-nine major indexes in its Stock Market Data Bank section. Certainly, many more lesser-known indexes are available.

2 You can also purchase preferred stock. Not as widely available, preferred shares generally carry no voting privileges. Further, preferred dividends are set at the time of issuance and don't have the upward potential common dividends do. A major advantage to preferred is that in the event of bankruptcy preferred shareholders will receive liquidation payment ahead of common holders.

3 If stocks aren't for you, investigate one of the many S&P indexed mutual funds.

4 For an excellent discussion of cyclical stocks, see Jordan E. Goodman and Sonny Bloch, *Everyone's Money Book* (Chicago: Dearborn Financial Publishing, Inc., 1997), p. 102.

5 "Sabre Holdings Corporation Added to S&P 500 Index," Press Release, Standard & Poor's, March 8, 2000.

6 These numbers, as calculated by The Conference Board, are preliminary because they have not undergone a final review. They are based on business cycle turning points from 1948 to 1999.

Notes: Chapter 8

1 For a discussion on the importance of income in applying for credit, see Jordan E. Goodman and Sonny Bloch, *Everyone's Money Book* (Chicago: Dearborn Financial Publishing, Inc., 1997), p. 395.

2 Jack R. Kapoor, Les R. Diabay, and Robert J. Hughes, *Personal Finance, 4th ed.* (Chicago: Irwin, 1996), p. 180.

3 Ibid.

4 The numbers, as calculated by The Conference Board, are preliminary because they have not undergone a final review. They are based on business cycle turning points from 1948 to 1999.

5 Chairman Alan Greenspan, "Remarks: The Challenge of Central Banking in a Democratic Society," the Federal Reserve Board, presented at the Annual Dinner and Francis Boyer Lecture of the American Enterprise Institute for Public Policy Research, Washington, D.C., December 5, 1996.

Notes: Chapter 9

1 "National Income and Product Accounts of the United States, 1929–94: Volume 1," U.S. Department of Commerce, April 1998, M-6.

2 "Gross Domestic Product: First Quarter 2000 (Final); Corporate Profits: First Quarter 2000 (Revised)," Press Release, U.S. Department of Commerce Bureau of Economic Analysis, June 29, 2000.

3 Consult the Survey of Current Business for a detailed breakdown of corporate profits. The publication is put out each month by the BEA and features national, regional, and international economic data. It is available at no charge online (www.bea.doc.gov/bea/pubs.htm) or for $48 a year by writing the U.S. Government Printing Office, Superintendent of Documents, Washington, D.C. 20402.

4 "Updated Summary NIPA Methodologies," Survey of Current Business, U.S. Department of Commerce Bureau of Economic Analysis, September 1998, p. 26.

5 E-mail interview with Kenneth A. Petrick, U.S. Department of Commerce Bureau of Economic Analysis. [March 18, 2000.]

6 "About BEA: BEA's Mission," U.S. Department of Commerce Bureau of Economic Analysis (www.bea.doc.gov/bea/role.htm), April 5, 2000, p. 1.

Notes: Chapter 10

1 Technically, banking institutions must keep federal funds based upon an average of reserves for a two-week period. Federal funds may fall below the average required amount on any day but will need to rise to meet the two-week average reserve calculation.

2 Actual reserve requirements for depository institutions as of December 30, 1999, are 3 percent on net transaction accounts up to $44.3 million and 10 percent on deposits more than $44.3 million.

3 Steven Vames, "Bond Market Soars After Cut in Interest Rate Between Fed Meetings Surprises Participants," The Wall Street Journal, October 16, 1998, C16.

4 The actual Federal Funds Rate depends on the interaction between the supply and demand for money. By buying and selling securities, the Federal Reserve can affect the available supply of money. However, the demand for money is determined by the banks' willingness to extend loans and the public's interest in these loans.

5 John C. Robertson and Daniel L. Thornton, "Using Federal Funds Futures Rates to Predict Federal Reserve Actions," Review, vol. 79, no. 6 (November/December 1997), p. 45.

6 "Prebon Yamane (U.S.A.) Inc. FOMC federal funds target rate 6.50% effective 5/16/2000."

7 Daniel L. Thornton, "Tests of the Market's Reaction to Federal Funds Rate Target Changes," *Review,* vol. 80, no. 6 (November/December 1998), p. 25.

Notes: Chapter 11

1 Joseph G. Haubrich and Ann M. Dombrosky, "Predicting Real Growth Using the Yield Curve," *Economic Review,* vol. 32, no.1 (1996 Quarter 1), p. 27.

2. See Dusan Stojanovic and Mark D. Vaughan, "Yielding Clues about Recessions: the Yield Curve as a Forecasting Tool," *The Regional Economist,* October 1997, pp. 10–11.

3 See the classic theoretical mathematical explanation of expectations hypothesis (long-term rates are the average of expected future short-term rates) by Frederic S. Mishkin, *The Economics of Money, Banking, and Financial Markets* (Boston: Little, Brown and Company, 1986), pp. 140–144.

4 The other segment of the national debt is non-marketable debt, which cannot be traded prior to maturity. An example would be the very familiar savings bonds. You cannot trade savings bonds with investors but you can cash them in at your bank before maturity.

Notes: Chapter 12

1 For a description of the changes in the new and old leading index see, "Details on the Revisions in the Composite Indexes," Business Cycle Indicators Overview, The Conference Board (www.tcb-indicators.org)1997, pp. 3–6.

2 "The Cyclical Indicator Approach," Business Cycle Indicators, The Conference Board, May 1997, p. 2.

3 Barry A. Beckman, "Reflections on BEA's Experience with Leading Economic Indicators," Business Cycle Indicators, The Conference Board, May 1997, p. 4.

4 "The Newly Revised Leading Index," Business Cycle Indicators Overview, The Conference Board (www.tcb-indicators.org), 1997, p. 7.

5 "The Cyclical Indicator Approach," Business Cycle Indicators, The Conference Board, January 2000, p. 2.

6 "Economic Indicators Increased 0.1% in March," *The Wall Street Journal,* May 5, 1999, A2.

7 "Leading Economic Indicators for December," Press Release, The Conference Board, February 2, 2000.

8 Beckman, pp. 3–4.

Bibliography

"About BEA: BEA's Mission." U.S. Department of Commerce Bureau of Economic Analysis (www.bea.doc.gov/bea/role.htm), April 5, 2000.

"Advance Report on Durable Goods Manufacturers' Shipments and Orders (June 2000)." Press Release, U.S. Department of Commerce Bureau of the Census, July 27, 2000.

Andrews, Robert, ed. Famous Lines: A Columbia Dictionary of Familiar Quotations. New York: Columbia University Press, 1997.

Beckman, Barry A. "Reflections on BEA's Experience with Leading Economic Indicators." Business Cycle Indicators, May 1997.

Boldin, Michael. "Mid-Year Review and Look Ahead." Business Cycle Indicators, August 1999.

Burns, Arthur F., and Wesley C. Mitchell. Measuring Business Cycles. NBER Studies in Business Cycles, no. 2 New York: National Bureau of Economic Research, 1946, report 1947.

"Business Cycle Chronology." NBER Reporter, Fall 1999.

Carnes, W. Stansbury, and Stephen D. Slifer. The Atlas of Economic Indicators: A Visual Guide to Market Forces and the Federal Reserve. New York: HarperCollins Publishers, 1991.

Clayton, Gary E., and Martin Gerhard Giesbrecht. A Guide to Everyday Economic Statistics. 3d ed. New York: McGraw-Hill, Inc., 1995.

"The Cyclical Indicator Approach." Business Cycle Indicators, January 2000.

"The Cyclical Indicator Approach." Business Cycle Indicators, May 1997.

"Details on the Revisions in the Composite Indexes." Business Cycle Indicators Overview, 1997.

Dreazen, Yochi J. "Labor Costs Continued to Climb in June." The Wall Street Journal, July 28, 2000, A2.

"Economic Indicators Increased 0.1% in March." The Wall Street

Journal, May 5, 1999, A2.

The Economist Guide to Economic Indicators: Making Sense of Economics. New York: John Wiley & Sons, Inc., 1997.

The Economist Numbers Guide: The Essentials of Business Numeracy. New York: John Wiley & Sons, Inc., 1997.

Ehrlich, Eugene, and Marshall De Bruhl, eds. The International Thesaurus of Quotations, 2d ed. New York: HarperCollins Publishers, Inc., 1996.

"ETA Mission Statement." U.S. Department of Labor Employment and Training Administration (www.doleta.gov/mission.htm), February 13, 2000.

"Fact Sheet—Unemployment Insurance." U.S. Department of Labor Employment and Training Administration (www.wdsc.org/layoff/ui.htm), February 13, 2000.

Fitzhenry, Robert I., ed. The Harper Book of Quotations, 3d ed. New York: HarperPerennial, 1983.

Goodman, Jordan E., and Sonny Bloch. Everyone's Money Book. Chicago: Dearborn Financial Publishing, Inc., 1997.

Goodman, Ted, ed. The Forbes Book of Business Quotations. New York: Black Dog & Leventhal Publishers, Inc., 1997.

Gottschalk, Earl C., Jr. "How Can You Tell a Bear Market Is Over?" *The Wall Street Journal*, October 22, 1990, C1.

Greenspan, Alan. "Remarks." The Federal Reserve Board, presented at the Fifteenth Anniversary Conference of the Center for Economic Policy Research (Stanford University, California), September 5, 1997.

Greenspan, Alan. "Remarks: The Challenge of Central Banking in a Democratic Society." The Federal Reserve Board, presented at the Annual Dinner and Francis Boyer Lecture of The American Enterprise Institute for Public Policy Research (Washington, D.C.), December 5, 1996.

Grimm, Bruce T., and Robert P. Parker. "Reliability of the Quarterly and Annual Estimates of GDP and Gross Domestic Income." Survey of Current Business, December 1998.

"Gross Domestic Product as a Measure of U.S. Production." Survey of Current Business, August 1991.

"Gross Domestic Product: First Quarter 2000 (Final); Corporate Profits: First Quarter 2000 (Revised)." Press Release, U.S. Department of Commerce Bureau of Economic Analysis, June 29, 2000.

Haubrich, Joseph G., and Ann M. Dombrosky. "Predicting Real Growth Using the Yield Curve." *Economic Review*, vol. 32, no. 1 (1996).

"Household Employer's Tax Guide (rev.), publication 926." Department of the Treasury, Internal Revenue Service, November 1999.

"Housing Starts and Building Permits in January 2000." Press Release, U.S. Department of Commerce Bureau of the Census, February 16, 2000.

"Housing Units Authorized by Building Permits." U.S. Department of Commerce Bureau of the Census (www.census.gov/const/www/C40/c40text.html), March 1, 2000.

Kapoor, Jack R., Les R. Diabay, and Robert J. Hughes. Personal Finance. 4th ed. Chicago: Irwin, 1996.

Lahiri, Kajal, and Geoffrey H. Moore, eds. Leading Economic Indicators: New Approaches and Forecasting Records. New York: Cambridge University Press, 1991.

"Leading Economic Indicators for December." Press Release, The Conference Board, February 2, 2000.

"Manufacturers' Shipments, Inventories, and Orders (M3) Survey." U.S. Department of Commerce, Bureau of the Census (www.census.gov/indicator/www/m3/m3desc.htm), February 26, 2000.

"Manufacturers' Shipments, Inventories, and Orders (M3): Technical Documentation U.S. Department of Commerce." U.S. Department of Commerce, Bureau of the Census, 1998.

Melicher, Ronald W., Merle T. Welshans, and Edgar A. Norton. Finance: Introduction to Institutions, Investments & Management. 9th ed. Cincinnati: South-Western Publishing Co., 1997.

"Minutes of the Federal Reserve Open Market Committee, November 17, 1998." The Federal Reserve Board (www.federalreserve.gov).

"Minutes of the Meeting of the Federal Open Market Committee Held on November 16, 1999." Federal Reserve Bulletin, February 2000.

Mishkin, Frederic S. The Economics of Money, Banking, and Financial Markets. Boston: Little, Brown and Company, 1986.

Mitchell, Wesley C. Business Cycles: The Problem and Its Settings. NBER Studies in Business Cycles, no. 1. New York: National Bureau of Economic Research, 1927, report 1949.

"Monetary Policy Report to Congress Submitted on February 17, 2000." Federal Reserve Bulletin, March 2000.

Moore, Geoffrey H. Business Cycles, Inflation, and Forecasting. 2d ed. Cambridge: Ballinger Publishing Co., 1983.

"National Income and Product Accounts of the United States, 1929–94: Volume 1." U.S. Department of Commerce, April 1998, M-6.

"The Newly Revised Leading Index." Business Cycle Indicators Overview, 1997.

Nicholson, Jonathan. "U.S. Housing Starts +1.5% to 1.775 Million Rate in January." Dow Jones News Service, February 16, 2000.

Poole, William. "That Mysterious FOMC." The Federal Reserve Board. Remarks before a meeting of The Economic Club of Memphis, Tennessee, December 3, 1998.

Robertson, John C., and Daniel L. Thornton. "Using Federal Funds Futures Rates to Predict Federal Reserve Actions," Review, vol. 79, no. 6 (November/December 1997).

Rogers, R. Mark. Handbook of Key Economic Indicators. 2d. ed. New York: McGraw-Hill, 1998.

"Sabre Holdings Corporation Added to S&P 500 Index," Press Release, Standard & Poor's, March 8, 2000.

Slavin, Steve. Economics: A Self-Teaching Guide. 2d ed. New York: John Wiley & Sons, Inc., 1999.

Stojanovic, Dusan, and Mark D. Vaughan. "Yielding Clues about Recessions: The Yield Curve as a Forecasting Tool." The Regional Economist, October 1997.

Stout, Hilary. "Durable-Goods Orders Fell 3.2% in June after 4.2% Gain." *The Wall Street Journal*, July 26, 1990, A2.

Tainer, Evelina M. Using Economic Indicators to Improve Investment Analysis. 2d ed. New York: John Wiley & Sons, Inc., 1998.

Thornton, Daniel L. "Tests of the Market's Reaction to Federal Funds Rate Target Changes." Review, vol. 80, no. 6 (November/December 1998).

"Unemployment Insurance Claims." U.S. Department of Labor Employment and Training Administration (www.doleta.gov/programs/claims.htm), February 13, 2000.

"Updated Summary NIPA Methodologies." Survey of Current Business, September 1998.

Vames, Steven. "Bond Market Soars after Cut in Interest Rate Between Fed Meetings Surprises Participants." *The Wall Street Journal*, October 16, 1998, C16.

Young, Allan H. "Reliability and Accuracy of the Quarterly Estimates of GDP." Survey of Current Business, October 1993.

Index

A

American Enterprise Institute for Public Policy Research, the, 94
Australia, 24

B

Bacon, Francis, 141
BEA, See Bureau of Economic Analysis
Beckman, Barry A., 151
big-ticket items, 1, 43, 48, 145
Board of Governors of the Federal Reserve Bank, 117
Boldin, Michael, 147
Bonaparte, Napoleon, 7
bond market, 2, 39, 67, 94, 111, 113, 114, 117, 125; interest rates, 113; maturity, 113
building permits, 1, 2, 8, 13, 55–68, 161
Bureau of Census, 50
Bureau of Economic Analysis, the, 8, 106, 108
Bureau of the Census, the, 7, 8, 51
business, 3; buying a small, 3
Business Cycle Dating Committee, 24
business cycle indicators, 104
business cycles, 142

C

C40 building permits, 64
Canada, 24
Carnegie, Andrew, 1
Census Bureau, the, 64, 65, 67, 106
Chase, Salmon P., 93
Chicago Tribune, the, 14, 27, 30, 41, 44, 53, 72, 82, 112, 125, 130, 137, 142, 154
Cleveland, Grover, 93
CNNfn, 14, 30, 41, 44, 53, 56, 68, 72, 82, 112, 125, 130, 137, 142, 153, 161
Commerce Department, the, 62
Conference Board, The, 9, 52, 73, 104, 146, 147, 148, 150
consumption, 20
Coolidge, Calvin, 13
corporate bonds, 122
corporate profits after tax, 1, 3, 5, 8, 13, 99–109, 161
Courier-Journal, 14, 27, 30, 41, 44, 53, 72, 82, 130, 137, 142, 154
current-production income, 103
cyclical stocks, 76
defensive stocks, 75

D

Denmark, 24
Department of Commerce, the, 106
Department of Defense, the, 50
dividends, 105, 106
Division of Labor, the, 35
Dombrosky, Ann M., 131
Dow Jones Industrial Average, the, 71
Dow Jones News Service, 62
downturn, 4, 16, 26, 48, 62, 67
durable goods, 20
durable goods orders, 1, 2, 7–8, 13, 43–53, 161; manufacturing activity, 43

E

economic benchmark, 13
Employment and Training Administration, the, 7, 35
England, 24
ETA. See Employment and Training Administration
expansion, 4, 6, 9, 14, 15, 16, 23, 24, 25, 32, 35, 45, 56, 62, 65, 66, 72, 74, 75, 81, 87, 88, 92, 99, 102, 143, 151, 152
expenditures, 21

F

federal funds, 3
federal funds rate, 1, 9, 13, 14, 111–126, 161
Federal Open Market Committee, the, 117, 118, 119, 124
Federal Reserve Bank of Cleveland's Economic Review, 131
Federal Reserve Bulletin, 91

Federal Reserve, the, 8, 9, 26, 85, 86, 87, 90, 91, 92, 93, 95, 96, 112, 113, 114, 116, 117, 118, 119, 125, 126, 132, 159
Ferguson Jr., Roger W., 111
forecasting indicators, 5; coincident, 5; lagging, 5; leading, 5
four-week average, 34

G

GDP. See gross domestic product
Germany, 19
GNP. See Gross National Product
government bonds, 122
Greenspan, Alan, 94, 117, 118, 119, 126, 159
gross domestic product, 4, 13–27, 100, 105, 106, 108, 118, 119, 141, 158
gross national product, 19
growth stocks, 74

H

Haubrich, Joseph G., 131
housing starts, 56, 65
Houston Chronicle, the, 14, 27, 41, 44, 53, 72, 82, 112, 125, 130, 137, 142, 154

I

income approach, 20
income stocks, 74
inflation, 13, 40, 67, 93, 118
interest rates, 87, 111
Internal Revenue Service, 106
international bonds, 122
investment, 20–21
Investor's Business Daily, 3, 14, 27, 30, 41, 44, 53, 57, 68,

72, 82, 86, 96, 100, 109, 112, 126, 130, 137, 142, 154, 161
Italy, 24

J
Japan, 19, 24
Juvenal, 99

L
leading economic indicator, 1, 3, 9, 13, 31, 56, 85, 141–154, 161
LEI. See leading economic indicator
Los Angeles Times, the, 14, 27, 41, 44, 53, 72, 82, 112, 125

M
M1 money , 90, 91
M2 money, 119
M2 money supply, 1, 3, 8, 13, 85–96, 146, 161
M3 money, 90, 91, 119
M3 report, 50, 51
Madison, James, 93
McKinley, William, 93
Miami Herald, the, 14, 27, 30, 41, 44, 53, 72, 82, 112, 125, 142, 154

N
NASDAQ. See National Association of Securities Dealers Automatic Quotation, the
National Association of Securities Dealers Automatic Quotation, the, 78
National Association of Securities Dealers, the, 78
National Bureau of Economic Research, the, 4, 15, 24

NBER. See National Bureau of Economic Research, the
net exports, 22
New York Stock Exchange, 71, 74, 78
New York Times, the, 14, 26, 30, 41, 44, 53, 56, 68, 72, 82, 100, 109, 112, 125, 130, 137, 142, 153, 161
nondurable goods, 20
nonresidential investments, 21
NYSE. See New York Stock Exchange

O
Oregonian, the, 14, 27, 44, 53, 72, 82, 112, 125, 130, 137, 142, 154
over-the-counter trading,, 78

P
part-time work, 33
peaks, 9, 16
Plato, 157

R
recession, 4, 8, 9, 14, 15, 16, 23, 24, 29, 31, 33, 38, 45, 46, 49, 50, 56, 65, 66, 71, 72, 75, 76, 79, 81, 86, 87, 88, 90, 92, 95, 99, 101, 102, 111, 125, 132, 137, 143, 144, 145, 147, 151, 152
refinancing, 3
residential investment, 21
Robertson, John C., 118
Rogers, Will, 71

S
S&P 100, 80
S&P 400 Mid Cap, 80
S&P 500, 1, 2, 8, 13, 71–82,

146, 161
S&P 500 Financial, 80
S&P 500 Industrials, 80
S&P 500 Transportation, 80
S&P 500 Utilities, 80
S&P 600 Small Cap, 80
S&P REIT Composite, 80
S&P SuperComposite 1500
    Index, 80
San Jose Mercury News, the,
    72, 82, 112, 125
Sandburg, Carl, 85
securities, 129; long-term, 129,
    130, 137; short-term, 129,
    130, 132, 134, 137
short-term bonds, 115
Slavin, Steve, 37, 38
Standard & Poor's Index. See
    S&P 500
stock market, 2, 39, 40, 52, 67,
    71, 73, 81, 90, 94, 124, 141,
    145
Stojanovic, Dusan, 132
Sweden, 24

T
Tampa Tribune, the, 72, 82,
    112, 125
Thornton, Daniel L., 118
three C's, 87
trough, 15, 16

U
U.S. Department of Labor, the,
    7
unemployment, 38; cyclical,
    38; frictional, 37, 38; struc-
    tural, 37, 38
unemployment compensation
    claims, 29–41
unemployment insurance
    claims, 1, 2, 7, 13, 14, 16, 161

Unemployment Insurance
    Weekly Claims Report, 35
upturns, 4, 26, 48, 62, 67
USA Today, 3, 14, 26, 44, 53,
    56, 68, 72, 82, 112, 125, 130,
    137, 142, 153, 161

V
Vaughan, Mark D., 132
Waldo Emerson, Ralph, 55

W
Wall Street, 5, 78, 132
Wall Street Journal, The, 3,
    14, 27, 30, 34, 41, 44, 49, 53,
    57, 68, 72, 82, 86, 96, 100,
    109, 112, 117, 118, 126, 130,
    134, 137, 142, 147, 150, 154,
    161
Washington Post, the, 14, 26,
    30, 41, 44, 53, 56, 68, 72, 82,
    100, 109, 112, 125, 130, 137,
    142, 153, 161

Y
yield curve, the, 1, 3, 9, 13,
    161, 129–138; downward-
    sloping, 131, 133, 137; flat,
    131; upward-sloping, 130,
    133, 137, 138

Z
zero-coupon bonds, 122

About the Author

Dr. Marie Bussing-Burks has an MBA and a doctorate in economics. She is an adjunct instructor of economics and finance at the University of Southern Indiana School of Business. She is also a Chartered Retirement Planning Specialist (CRPS) and is the author of numerous magazine, newspaper and journal articles, and textbook chapters. Her work has appeared in such publications as *Health & Money, Economic Facts,* and *The American Economist.* Bussing-Burks has also reviewed books on economics, business, and politics. She delivers conference papers to the National Association of Economic Educators, the MidSouth Academy of Economics and Finance, the Southwestern Society of Economics, and others. She lives in Evansville, Indiana, with her family.